STP® STANDARD IN MOST $300,000 CARS.

When a machine this powerful, finely tuned, and expensive rolls onto the track, STP Oil Treatment is standard equipment.

3 out of 4 Indy car drivers use STP. In the most demanding situations found on asphalt.

So when an Indy driver feels a slap on the back from several hundred horsepower, accompanied by a high-rpm shriek from an engine inches behind his helmet, he can take comfort in this fact: His engine has been meticulously prepared. And the checklist includes STP Oil Treatment.

Nothing less than painstaking preparation is needed to survive a 500 mile ordeal like Indianapolis.

And among top finishers at Indy this year, a telling 7 out of 10 were STP users.

Which should send a message to all drivers about standard equipment they should consider for next year: STP.

B FIRST BRANDS

THE PPG PACE CAR TEAM... Leading the Way

High-tech, high performance, specially built pace cars were again featured in this year's PPG fleet, along with a brilliantly designed GMC pace truck. Among the featured marques were **Buick Regal GNX, Cadillac Allanté, Chevrolet Camaro, Chevrolet Corvette, Dodge M4S, Ford SVO Mustang, Oldsmobile Calais,** and **Ferrari**.

Not as visible as this unique vehicle collection and the highly attractive team of lady race drivers at their wheels is the $2.325 million in prize money posted for the 1988 PPG Indy Car World Series. $2.16 million of this fund, the largest for any autoracing series, is distributed as prize money and PPG Cup funds in the CART series. Another $165,000 goes to the Indianapolis 500, where PPG is the largest individual sponsor.

The entire program, one of the most comprehensive in the field of motorsports is, overseen with his trademark efficiency and geniality by Jim Chapman, PPG's Director of Racing

THE PPG PACE CAR DRIVERS

DEBRA MAYER Debra started racing motorcycles (Moto-Cross) in 1974. She next raced Formula Fords in SCCA regional and national competition with her highest finish third. In 1987, she competed in the Skip Barber Midwest Racing Series.

TRISHA HESSINGER Trisha has been an accomplished figure skater since age three and is now a professional figure skating coach in her home town of Allentown, PA. She has competed successfully with Formula Fords in the Skip Barber Series, winning several events. Trisha also instructs high speed driving for Pocono International Raceway.

KATHY RUDE In 1982, Kathy became the first woman to win a professional road race in America, when her team finished first in the GTU class at IMSA's 24 Hours at Daytona. She had earned recognition as one of the top women drivers in the world when a serious accident at Brainerd, MN, in 1983 interrupted her career. Kathy is now fully recovered and able to continue in her fifth year with the pace car team. Seattle-based Kathy is married to driver Ludwig Heimrath, who competes in the PPG Indy Car World Series.

DESIRÉ WILSON Desiré, the only Indy Car driver on the team, has raced in 11 Indy Car events, with a finish as high as 10th. Her lap of 191 mph in 1982 at Indianapolis still stands as the fastest lap ever run there by a woman. Desiré, is the only woman ever to win a Formula One race (Brands Hatch in 1980). She has won two World Endurance Sports Car races and 17 other professional races, with 74 Top Three finishes and 11 pole positions.

MARGIE SMITH-HAAS Margie, who began her auto racing career while teaching school in Phoenix, has raced largely in IMSA GTO and endurance events. In both 1984 and 1985, she was the only woman driver competing in the 24 Hours at LeMans.

ALICE RIDPATH Alice won the South Florida Solo II championship in both 1978 and 1979 and has three national victories in SCCA road racing events. She was runner-up for the 1985 championship in the Southeast Division of SCCA. In 1986, she competed in the Escort Endurance Series and in 1987 raced in IMSA's Firehawk Series, where she plans to continue.

JANEY SMITH A resident of Santa Cruz, CA, Janey began her career in racing as a crew member, then an SCCA official, before entering competition as a driver in 1984.

JODI DANGEL Jodi started driving competitively in 1982 with the Porsche Club of America. She holds professional licenses in both SCCA and IMSA and in 1986 drove in the SCCA VW Golf Cup Series and the IMSA Champion Spark Plug Challenge Series, competing against her husband, Jeff.

PATTY MOISE Patty made motorsports history in 1986 at Portland International Raceway when she became the first woman to achieve an overall individual victory in a professional road race. In 1986, she finished second in IMSA's American Challenge Series. In 1987, Patty competed in her Buick in NASCAR's Busch Grand National Series, becoming the first woman to win an event at Martinsville (VA) Speedway.

ROBIN McCALL-DALLENBACH Robin began driving quarter midgets at age eight, drove her first stock car race at age 14. At age 18, she won 10 of 17 feature events at San Antonio Speedway. In 1987, she finished fourth in points in the American Challenge Series, driving an Oldsmobile Tornado. Her husband, Wally Dallenbach, Jr., is a former Trans-Am champion and sometime Indy Car driver.

*LYN ST. JAMES Lyn began her 1987 racing season with a bang, driving a Ford Mustang to victory in the GTO Division at IMSA's 24 Hours at Daytona with co-drivers Bill Elliott and Tom Gloy. In 1985, she became the fastest woman driver in history when she sped a Ford Probe GTP around the Alabama International Motor Speedway at 204.223 mph, establishing 13 closed course records during speed trials at the Talledega track.

*SANDRA BARTLEY Sandra is a native of Toronto but now a movie/TV actress in California. She began racing in 1976 with the Southern California Porsche Club and has won championships in three different divisions in seven of the past eight years, driving time trials, slaloms and rallies.

* not shown

Cadillac Allanté leads an outstanding lineup of PPG Pace Cars. First ever Pace Truck, a brilliantly hued GMC Sierra, does double duty as transport for television crew.

MARTINI & ROSSI/LANCIA
THE WORLD CHAMPIONS REPEAT

Martini & Rossi/Lancia won its third World Rally Championship, its second in a row when Miki Biasion romped home first in the Rally d'Italia. Additionally this made Biasion the World Rally Champion, the first Italian driver to win a world driving title in 35 years. Among his other victories on the circuit was the Olympus Rally, the only World Championship Rally in the U.S. Lancia's Delta Integrale rally cars dominated the series this year.

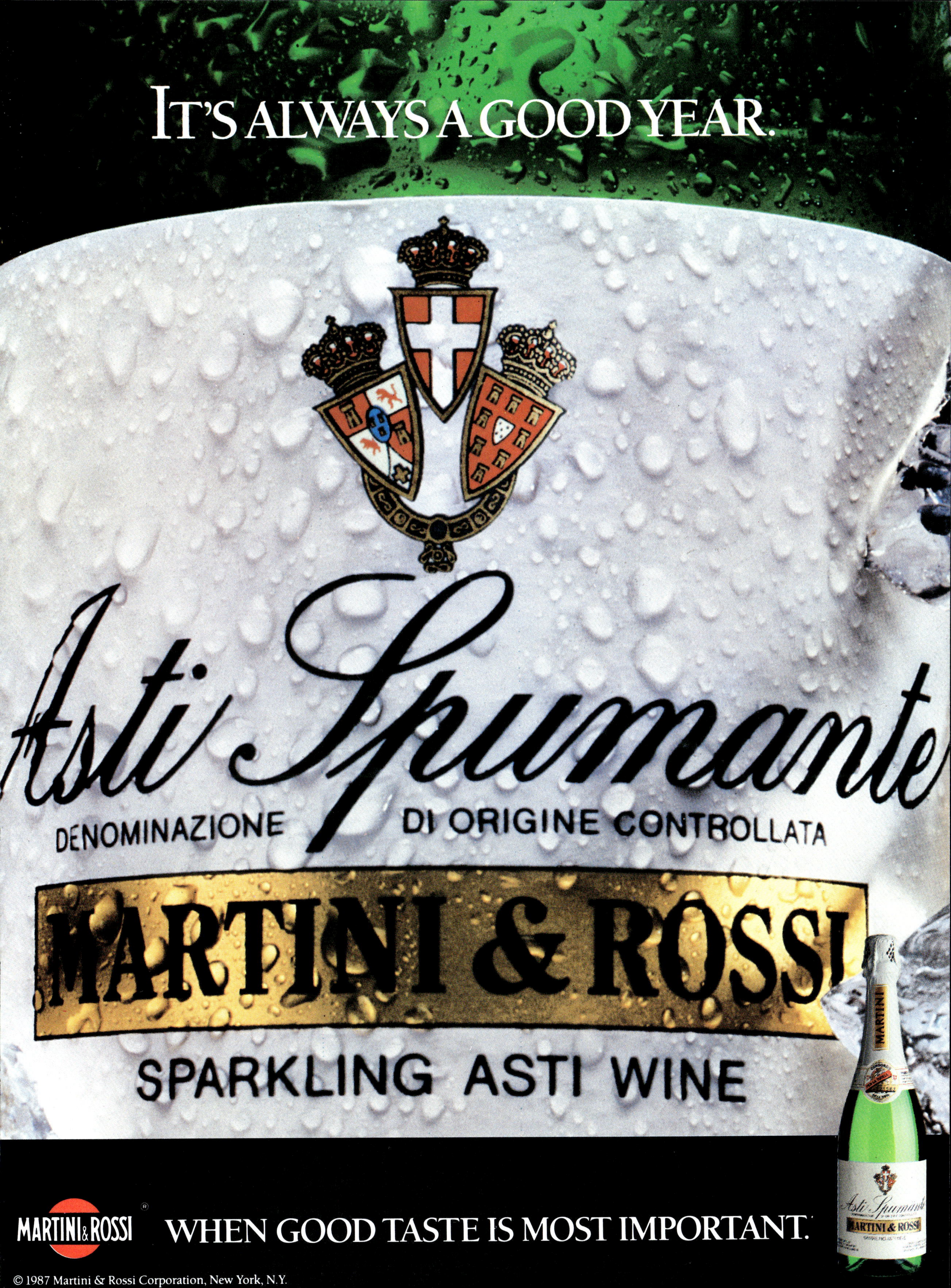
IT'S ALWAYS A GOOD YEAR.
Asti Spumante
DENOMINAZIONE DI ORIGINE CONTROLLATA
MARTINI & ROSSI
SPARKLING ASTI WINE
MARTINI & ROSSI
WHEN GOOD TASTE IS MOST IMPORTANT.
© 1987 Martini & Rossi Corporation, New York, N.Y.

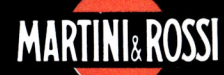

CONTENTS

2 The PPG Pace Car Team, Leading the Way
11 Drivers, by David Phillips
17 Drivers, '88 Individual Records
85 Teams, by David Phillips
92 Events, 15 Races Counting Toward the PPG Cup
105 Jim Crawford, Raw Courage in the Indianapolis Arena, by Mike Harris
133 The Technical Side, by J. Kirk Russell
136 Chevrolet Indy V8 Takes 14 of 15 CART/PPG Races
139 Danny Sullivan, The Champion Takes a Cool-Off Lap, by Jon Saraceno
144 A.J. Foyt, A Super Season for Super Tex, by Mike Harris
146 Al Holbert's Quaker State Porsche Team, by Lewis Franck
148 Andy Kenopensky, A Team Owner with 80,000 Shareholders, by Jan Shaffer
149 Tony Bettenhausen, by Brian Muir
150 Out of the Cockpit, Dick Simon's New Career, by Lewis Franck
154 Pit Parade
164 CART Family
166 For the Record
168 CART Awards Banquet
174 '89 Outlook for Indy Car Racing
186 Valvoline Championship for Bosch-Volkswagen Super Vee
189 International Race of Champions
190 HFC American Racing Series
191 HFC Formula Atlantic
192 $1 Million Corvette Challenge

Publisher: John Norwood
Associate Publisher: Barbara A. Hassler
Art Director: Robert Steig
Editor: Jonathan Hughes
Statistics: John Evenson, CART
Photographic Team: Bill Stahl (who took the dust jacket photograph) and Dan Bianchi, Chief Photographers; Dan R. Boyd, Chief Photographer, CART; Ron McQueeney, Chief Photographer Indianapolis Motor Speedway; Steve Swope

Photographs have been contributed by Art Flores, Michael C. Brown, Bobby Steig, Janice O'Rourke, Indianapolis Motor Speedway, Schulman/MWN&S, Creative Images, Rogers & Cowan, Inc., Gridwork, and Chevrolet in addition to the Photographic Team listed. CART's John Evenson was again an appreciated contributor.

CART 88/89 is published by Autosport International, Inc., 79 Madison Avenue, New York, NY 10016. © 1988 by Autosport International, Inc. No part may be reproduced without prior written permission.

Distributed in the U.S. by Motorbooks International, Osceola, WI 54020

In coveralls or pinstripes, the team to beat is Penske and Rolex.

On a speedway or in a boardroom, winning is what Roger Penske does best.

In the early Sixties, he was one of the country's leading professional road-racing drivers. By the time he was 25, Penske had won so many races he was twice named driver of the year.

But his greatest victories have been won in pinstripes. Today he is president and chief executive officer of Penske Corporation, an over two-billion-dollar transportation services conglomerate.

He steered it from a single auto dealership to a corporation employing more than 9500 people in 37 states and England.

However, the name on the executive suite still carries off the checkered flag. Penske personally manages the racing team he founded, and with seven wins at Indy, he holds the all-time record for an owner.

A man who prevails over every challenge and exceeds each demand for exacting performance, Roger Penske is unique in his universe.

How well-teamed, indeed, the man is with his timepiece. Rolex.

ROLEX

Day-Date, Oyster Perpetual, President are trademarks.

Day-Date Oyster Perpetual Chronometer in 18 kt. gold and matching President bracelet.

Write for brochure. Rolex Watch U.S.A., Inc., Dept. 584, Rolex Building, 665 Fifth Avenue, New York, New York 10022-5383.
© 1985 Rolex Watch U.S.A., Inc.

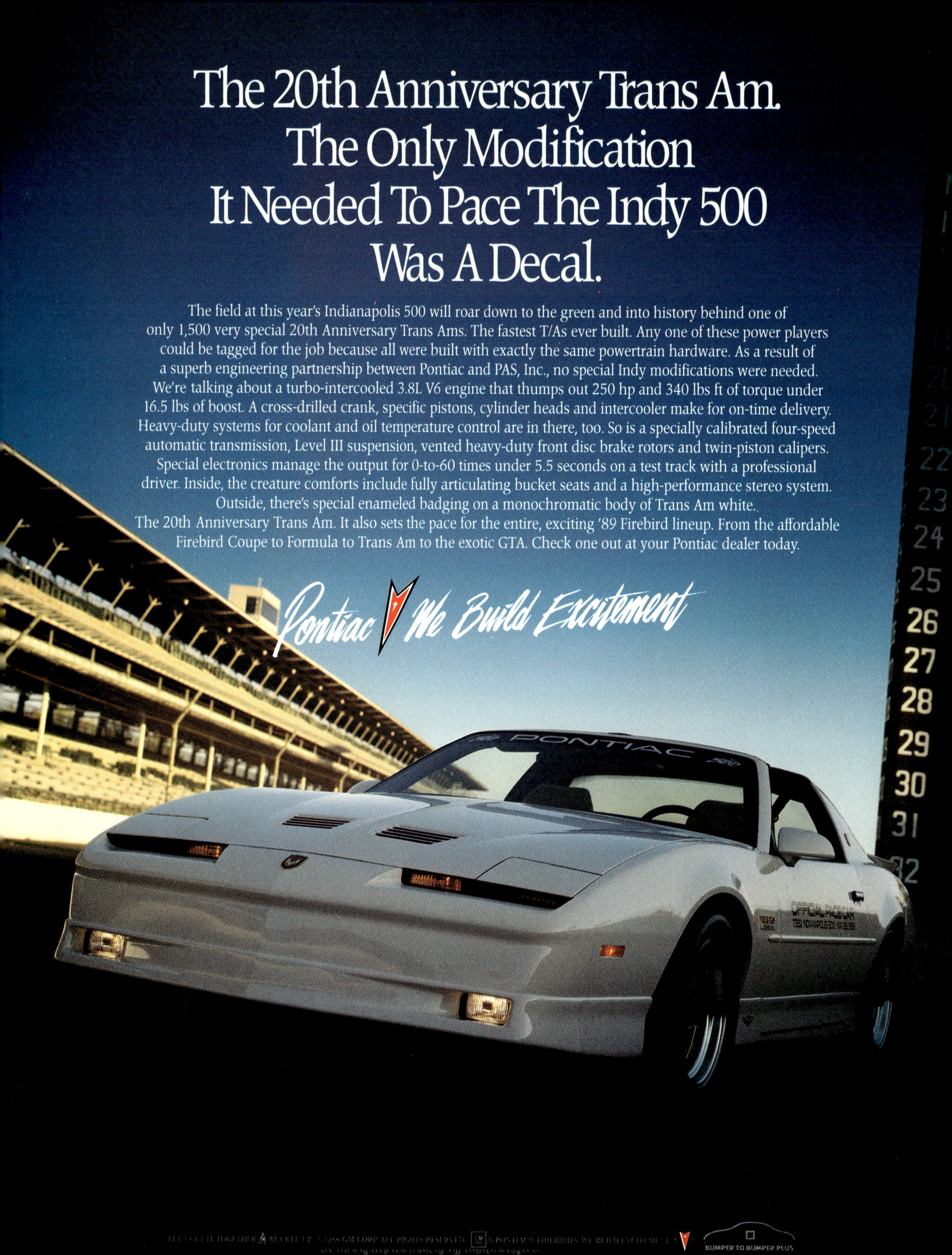

The 20th Anniversary Trans Am.
The Only Modification
It Needed To Pace The Indy 500
Was A Decal.
The field at this year's Indianapolis 500 will roar down to the green and into history behind one of only 1,500 very special 20th Anniversary Trans Ams. The fastest T/As ever built. Any one of these power players could be tagged for the job because all were built with exactly the same powertrain hardware. As a result of a superb engineering partnership between Pontiac and PAS, Inc., no special Indy modifications were needed.
We're talking about a turbo-intercooled 3.8L V6 engine that thumps out 250 hp and 340 lbs ft of torque under 16.5 lbs of boost. A cross-drilled crank, specific pistons, cylinder heads and intercooler make for on-time delivery. Heavy-duty systems for coolant and oil temperature control are in there, too. So is a specially calibrated four-speed automatic transmission, Level III suspension, vented heavy-duty front disc brake rotors and twin-piston calipers. Special electronics manage the output for 0-to-60 times under 5.5 seconds on a test track with a professional driver. Inside, the creature comforts include fully articulating bucket seats and a high-performance stereo system. Outside, there's special enameled badging on a monochromatic body of Trans Am white.
The 20th Anniversary Trans Am. It also sets the pace for the entire, exciting '89 Firebird lineup. From the affordable Firebird Coupe to Formula to Trans Am to the exotic GTA. Check one out at your Pontiac dealer today.
Pontiac We Build Excitement
PONTIAC
OFFICIAL PACE CAR
BUMPER TO BUMPER PLUS

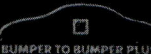

DRIVERS...

By David Phillips

Perhaps Danny Sullivan will get a little respect now. Despite the fact that he'd won seven Indy Car races in the past four seasons, far too many fans and self-styled experts preferred to focus on Danny's well-publicized social agenda rather than his racing exploits. Perhaps that's why in a pre-race poll of some fifty reporters, only one favored Danny to win the Indianapolis 500 and why, after the race, an unknowing fan smugly proclaimed on television that Sullivan had "choked."

No, Danny did not "choke" at Indianapolis or any other race. After a frustrating start to the season, Sullivan headed to Milwaukee lying 23rd in the CART/PPG Cup standings with two whole championship points. From Milwaukee onward, however, he finished nine of ten races in the top five and, at Mid-Ohio, took over the points lead for keeps. Along the way, Sullivan started more than half of the races from pole and, when his sometimes finicky Penske PC-17 was right, the only thing that could beat him on Sunday was the odd mechanical failure or the unavoidable mishap. And in the end, Sullivan clinched his first racing title in fitting style, but for pit stops leading all the way at Laguna Seca to claim his fourth win of the year. Together with his other victories at Portland, Michigan and Nazareth that gives Danny eleven wins in five years, six of which, by the way, have come on ovals.

Al Unser, Jr. also answered his critics in 1988, especially anyone who intimated he hadn't given his all at Shierson Racing last year or who questioned the hefty retainer Rick Galles is said to have paid him to return to the Albuquerque-based team. All Al did was win four races in a March 88C, a chassis that some of the world's most celebrated drivers—men like Emerson Fittipaldi, Michael Andretti and Raul Boesel—abandoned in frustration by mid-season.

Unser gave early notice that he would be a force to be reckoned with by whistling through the field from an indifferent grid spot at Phoenix to close on the leaders before his engine was felled by oil scavenging problems. Although Al qualified third at Long Beach, it was little indication of his race day strength, where he simply demolished the field on the way to a full lap victory.

Thus the pattern was established. Al, who has yet to gain his first Indy Car pole, would routinely qualify somewhere on the second or third row and charge like a hungry lion on race day. On the road courses and street circuits, where the disadvantages of the March 88C could be offset by pure driving talent, Unser was magnificent. In fact, his temporary circuit record was virtually spotless, failing to win only at Cleveland and he finished the season as the runaway leader in road/temporary circuit points and prize money. Of course, no discussion of Unser's 1988 season would be complete without some mention of "the incident" at the Meadowlands, in which Al and Emerson Fittipaldi banged together while fighting for the lead, sending Fittipaldi on a one way trip into the wall. Much has been written of Unser's boldness or, as some prefer, recklessness on that fateful lap. The fact remains, that Al DID get squarely alongside of Fittipaldi on the entrance to the chicane. More importantly, Al was completely in control of his car at the time—this was no banzai move where caution was thrown to the wind. It was a typically hard-nosed, calculated move on a track where one had to make the most of his passing opportunities.

Although Bobby Rahal was denied in his bid to become the first man since Ted Horn to win three straight national titles, 1988 further enhanced his standing as one of the most complete drivers in Indy Car competition. Handicapped early-on by a somewhat anemic early season Judd powerplant, Rahal nevertheless scored steadily before coming to the fore in dramatic fashion at Cleveland, finishing a close second after losing the lead on a late bobble in traffic on a crumbling track.

From Cleveland on, Bobby was usually in with a chance and won the carnage-filled Pocono 500 to take the lead in the championship against all odds. But fate would extract its revenge a couple of weeks later, when Rahal was punted into the guardrail at Mid-Ohio by the spinning Ludwig Heimrath. While Bobby was able to gain ground on Sullivan at Road America, the rash of blistered tires at Nazareth all but ended his championship hopes.

By that time, of course, Bobby had announced his celebrated move to Kraco Racing for the 1989 season. It is some measure of the man that he remained as focused as ever on the job at hand, earnestly striving to bring a third title to the family and team that had nurtured him from a struggling driver to a true champion.

You could hardly call Rick Mears' season a disappointing one. After all, there was a third Indy 500 win, a follow-up victory at Milwaukee, fourth in the points race, number one in earnings and, on the intangible side, the satisfaction of besting Mario Andretti in three eyeball-to-eyeball confrontations for the pole at Indy, Michigan and Pocono.

And yet, despite all the success, one can't help but wonder whether this was a championship that got away from Mears. In the hyper-competitive world of Indy Car racing, few teams enjoy a significant mechanical advantage often or for long. And this year, the Penske PC-17 was clearly the car to have. No doubt Rick would like to have Phoenix to do over again; he'd think twice about trying to put a second lap on Randy Lewis around the outside of Turn Four and go on to run away with the race as he had for the first twenty-two miles. Michigan and Pocono were two more that got away, thanks to mechanical problems. While there's no guarantee that Rick could have beaten Sullivan at Nazareth had the Pennzoil PC-17 not blistered its tires, nobody would turn down a sure 16 points in a close title race in late September.

Mario Andretti continued to set the standard of excellence, on and off track. He came through to a somewhat fortunate win at Phoenix, profiting from Mears' shunt, Luyendyk's pit fire and some timely pit stops. But he flat out whipped Rahal and Sullivan at Cleveland on a day in which chassis set-up and horsepower were less a factor than guile and guts. The legendary bad Andretti luck continued to plague Mario at times, costing him a certain win at the Meadowlands. If Mears would like another shot at Phoenix, Mario would surely be up for another go at Pocono, where he slammed the wall while leading after tangling with Dick Simon.

Having come a close second the past two years, Michael Andretti could only win the title or face further frustration. From the outset of the season it was apparent that the sands of time had finally run out for the standard issue Cosworth DFX. Although Michael took a brilliant pole at Milwaukee, he didn't lead a single lap until Portland. A switch to the Lola chassis at Michigan helped some, but by then Michael was well into negotiations about his future and it didn't involve Kraco Racing. Like his nemesis Rahal, who ironically will replace him at Kraco, Michael never stopped giving anything less than 110%. However it wasn't until the new short stroke Cosworth arrived on the scene in September that he returned to serious contention. With his 1989 deal to join his father at Newman/Haas complete, he went to Tamiami Park with an untroubled

Ladies, Start Your Engines!

Ten members of the PPG Pace Car Team stand beside the fleet of PPG pace cars which they drive in parade laps at the start of each race in the PPG Indy Car Wold Series and in precision drills during race weekends. One of these specially built pace cars is selected to serve as the official pace car at each race, remaining on the track to pace the race after the other vehicles peel off at the end of the parade laps. Front row, left to right, are Margie Smith-Haas, Trisha Hessinger, Kathy Rude, Patty Moise, and Robin McCall-Dallenbach; back row, left to right, are Debbie Mayer, Desiré Wilson, Jane Smith, Jodi Dangel and Alice Ridpath.

Oh, Danny (Sullivan) Boy, Irish Eyes Are Smiling!

PPG tips its racing cap to the champion of the 1988 PPG Indy Car World Series

You did it, Danny, racing full steam ahead all season to win the PPG Cup, symbolic of the championship of the world's richest racing series.

And your victory was a tribute to the competence and perseverance of Roger Penske, owner of your Penske PC-17, as well as to your sponsor, Miller High Life, and the outstanding crew of designers, car builders, engineers and mechanics behind the scenes.

In a series that demands remarkable versatility for driving the world's fastest racing machines on super-speedways, short ovals, winding road courses and temporary street circuits, you demonstrated the skills and courage that mark a true champion.

And your car, like the entire starting field at all races in the series, was painted with PPG's tough urethane finishes.

Proving once again why PPG automotive finishes are the number one choice of automotive manufacturers worldwide.

mind and promptly garnered the top spot in the Marlboro Challenge to end his five year association with Maurice Kraines on a typically winning note.

Emerson Fittipaldi was the last of the two-time winners, prevailing at Mid-Ohio and Road America to match Mears and Mario in this critical department. While the Road America triumph was largely a tactical victory, with fuel economy playing the dominant role, Mid-Ohio was a tour-de-force. Emmo out drove, out engineered, out thought and out guessed the competition on an afternoon of constantly changing conditions at one of North America's trickiest circuits. But there were other, non-winning, drives worthy of note as well, principally Indianapolis. At Indy Fittipaldi patiently waited for the race to come back to him and beat everyone but Mears.

If Emerson matched Rick and Mario in the win column, he also matched them in the wish column, for the Meadowlands is a race that Fittipaldi would surely like to run again. Had Emerson shut the door earlier or simply let Al through and tried to regain the lead at some later time, the most it would have cost him was four points. Like Unser, however, Fittipaldi knew that there were no second chances at the Meadowlands.

Raul Boesel and Derek Daly finished the year eighth and ninth in the standings, respectively. In equally matched Lola-Cosworths, Raul and Derek each started the season with high expectations only to find their Cosworths simply weren't up to the job of finishing in the top three with any consistency, let alone winning races. Boesel put up a number of gritty performances, and while his best finish of the season was a fourth at Long Beach, few would argue that his finest hours came in the rain at Mid-Ohio and in the Marlboro Challenge. After problems in qualifying consigned him to 26th on the grid at Mid-Ohio, Raul drove a fabulous race, coming to fifth after ten laps and finishing sixth. Similarly, he hauled the Domino's Pizza entry up to third in the Marlboro Challenge, and might have figured even higher but for a broken third gear.

Daly was plagued by bad luck much of the season, dropping out of an Indianapolis 500 in which he could well have played a prominent role when his gearbox broke. He sprinted from eighth to fifth in the first lap at Milwaukee before insurmountable handling problems dropped him to eleventh. Then there was a coming together with Randy Lewis at Portland followed by a first lap crash with John Andretti at the Meadowlands. Even his best finish of the year—a fourth at Pocono—was tinged with disappointment in that Roberto Guerrero pipped him for third on the final lap.

Tenth place in total points was the joint property of two "rookies of the year." One, Teo Fabi, won the award for his brilliant 1984 season. The other, John Jones won the '88 title, the first annual Jim Trueman trophy, and its $50,000 "honorarium" after a year of steady development and increasing speed. Fabi, of course, moved into the Quaker State Porsche after several years in Formula One. Although the results weren't what Fabi, the team and Porschefiles the world over might have hoped, it was certainly not for want of trying on Teo's part. Anyone who had the pleasure of watching Fabi hustle the March-Porsche around the streets of Toronto could see a man getting the last possible hundredth of a second from a race car. A week later and there was Teo on the provisional pole at the Meadowlands and it seemed justice was being served. But Teo was destined to finish the Meadowlands race by the wayside and thereafter, as he had the first part of year, the quiet Italian had to be content with picking-up the odd fourth or fifth.

Jones began the year somewhat unsteadily, dropping out at Phoenix and Long Beach and failing to make the show at Indy. But he would rebound from that dismal month of May beginning at Portland. Having realized just how hard Indy Car racing can be at the Brickyard and Milwaukee he was glad to be able to put that effort to use on a road circuit again. Through the summer he amassed a string of top seven placings, culminated by a great drive in the sloppy Mid-Ohio outing where he gave nothing away to the likes of Sullivan, Boesel, and Fabi.

The final standings give little indication of the kind of season experienced by Arie Luyendyk and his sometime Simon Racing comrade Didier Theys. Luyendyk was remarkable through the first half of the year, leading at Phoenix and heading the pursuit of Sullivan at Indianapolis before almost getting that elusive first win with a brilliant drive at Portland. But crashes at the Meadowlands and Pocono crippled Simon's effort financially and left Arie physically hobbled. It wasn't until Miami that the free-spirited Dutchman regained his earlier form. Theys finished his road course-only season with a third at Miami, the placing coming as much from attrition among the other front runners as speed. Cleveland, Toronto and the Meadowlands were truer tests of the Belgian's talents. While glitzy finishes eluded him there, he ran ahead of the likes of Boesel and Daly.

On the downside, Roberto Guerrero had a nightmarish season, made doubly horrific by the fleeting promise with which it began. Nobody would have blamed Roberto had he worked his way back into Indy Car racing gradually following his near fatal accident in September, 1987. But there he was, sitting on the outside of the front row at Phoenix and, later, going wheel to wheel with Michael Andretti in as stern a test of resolve as the sport has to offer. But the miraculous second at Phoenix was followed by a curiously uncompetitive Long Beach and a first lap accident at Indy in which Guerrero was utterly blameless. Roberto's (as well as the team's) shortcomings in chassis set-up became increasingly obvious following the post-Indy departure of engineer Lee Dykstra. While he later finished third at Pocono after a two race sabbatical, Guerrero and his team were unable to reproduce the magic in their '87 partnership.

Al Unser made five races, including appearances in the 500 mile events with Penske Racing and two guest spots with Vince Granatelli at Toronto and the Meadowlands. To nobody's surprise, Al was a potential winner in all three 500s and desperately unlucky not to win both Michigan and Pocono. His stint at Granatelli simply proved that more was amiss with that team than its driver.

Kevin Cogan also had a day or two in the sun, despite missing the heart of the season after shattering his left arm in a crash at the Toronto race. Before that, he had driven superbly at Long Beach and only lost out on a battle for second with Rahal when his March 87C proved too thirsty. Upon his return, he went superbly again at Road America—when his car was running. He finished the year with useful runs at Laguna Seca and Tamiami Park.

John Andretti also missed part of the season due to injury, and the final two races due to the demise of his team. Otherwise, young John was repeatedly victimized by poor reliability, losing several potential top three finishes to mechanical failures. Although he was less of a force on the road courses, he figured in every oval race. These included Phoenix, where he dueled with Guerrero and cousin Michael, Milwaukee, where he battled uncle Mario, Michigan and Pocono. At the latter he looked set for a top five finish before his titanic pit lane accident.

Lost among the statistics, three more drives stand-out above the rest. Jim Crawford made a dramatic return to Indianapolis to offer the most serious challenge of the day to the Penske cars. He appeared to have a lock on the top three before a late pit stop for a punctured tire. Rocky Moran, surely one of the most underrated drivers in the land, drove Gohr Racing's monoplane March 87C to a great sixth at Long Beach. Then there was Scott Pruett, who spent a large portion of his life savings to run with Simon Racing at Long Beach. He later filled-in quite capably for Kevin Cogan at the Meadowlands and, in particular, Mid-Ohio. Hot on the scent of the recently vacated Truesports seat, Pruett ran three races at two tracks (the others being a Trans-Am at Mid-Ohio and an IMSA GTO race at Lime Rock). He turned in a spectacular performance in the CART race that saw him battling the vastly more experienced Boesel for fifth before a spin into the guardrail. Perhaps as a result, Scott landed the prized Truesports ride for 1989. If he does well we may have a Hollywood scenario to match Al Unser's trip from a spectator's seat to victory circle in the 1987 Indianapolis 500.

Galles RACING

1988 Indy Car Wins: Long Beach, Toronto, Meadowlands, and Miami.

**Thanks to the rest of our Winning Team,
OUR 1988 SPONSORS.**

Valvoline, Stroh, Raychem, Chevrolet, Bosch,
Excide Battery, Goodyear, PPG, Foot Joy,
Red Lion Inns, Valvoline Instant Oil Change,
and Galles Chevrolet.

Galles Racing   P.O. Box 25047   Albuquerque, New Mexico 87125

PPG INDY CAR WORLD SERIES

EVENT	START	FINISH	PURSE	POINTS	TOTAL
Checker 200/Phoenix	8	23	$ 13,830	0	0
Toyota Grand Prix of Long Beach	1	13	27,300	1	1
Indianapolis 500	2	23	214,378	1	2
Miller High Life 200/Milwaukee	5	2	38,280	16	18
Budweiser/G.I. Joe's 200/Portland	1	1	77,660	21	39
Budweiser Cleveland Grand Prix	1	3	34,500	16	55
Molson Indy/Toronto	1	2	62,880	17	72
Marlboro Grand Prix/Meadowlands	4	4	44,960	12	84
Marlboro 500/Michigan	5	1	111,196	20	104
Quaker State 500/Pocono	2	18	16,547	0	104
Escort Radar Warning 200/Mid-Ohio	1	5	31,840	11	115
Briggs & Stratton 200/Elkhart Lake	1	4	29,960	13	128
Bosch Grand Prix/Nazareth	1	1	52,460	21	149
Champion 300km/Laguna Seca	1	1	59,660	22	171
Nissan Indy Challenge/Miami	1	5	35,340	11	182

1 Danny Sullivan

PPG INDY CAR WORLD SERIES

EVENT	START	FINISH	PURSE	POINTS	TOTAL
Checker 200/Phoenix	4	18	$ 13,830	0	0
Toyota Grand Prix of Long Beach	4	1	91,160	21	21
Indianapolis 500	5	13	111,753	0	21
Miller High Life 200/Milwaukee	4	20	18,080	0	21
Budweiser/G.I. Joe's 200/Portland	4	4	40,460	12	33
Budweiser Cleveland Grand Prix	10	4	28,460	12	45
Molson Indy/Toronto	3	1	73,160	21	66
Marlboro Grand Prix/Meadowlands	6	1	91,160	20	86
Marlboro 500/Michigan	6	21	21,134	0	86
Quaker State 500/Pocono	11	2	57,539	16	102
Escort Radar Warning 200/Mid-Ohio	2	4	32,460	12	114
Briggs & Stratton 200/Elkhart Lake	3	7	23,600	6	120
Bosch Grand Prix/Nazareth	6	19	18,080	0	120
Champion 300km/Laguna Seca	3	6	28,220	8	128
Nissan Indy Challenge/Miami	5	1	64,160	21	149

2 Al Unser, Jr.

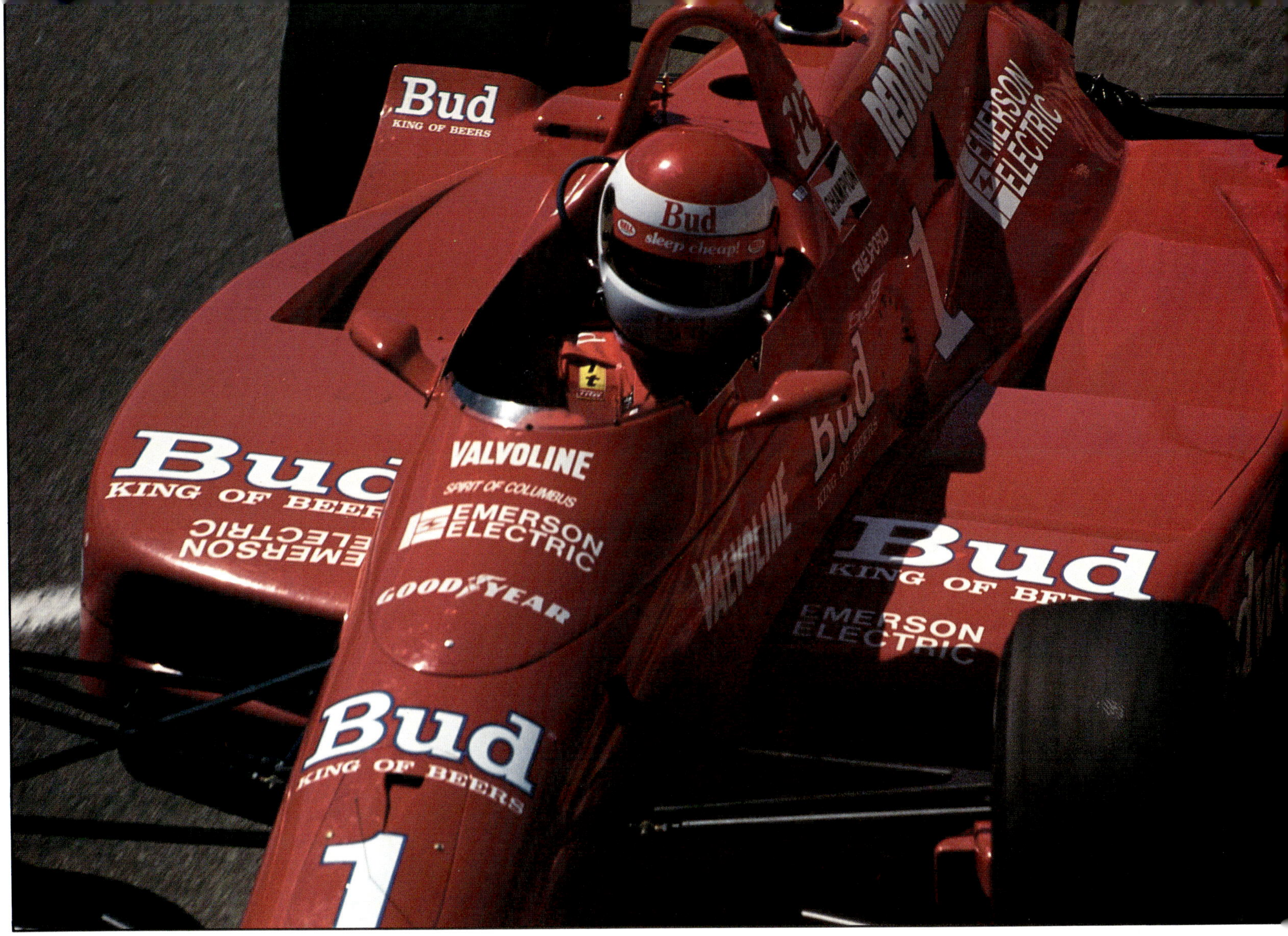

3 Bobby Rahal

EVENT	START	FINISH	PURSE	POINTS	TOTAL
Checker 200/Phoenix	12	16	$ 13,830	0	0
Toyota Grand Prix of Long Beach	8	2	74,180	16	16
Indianapolis 500	19	5	151,453	10	26
Miller High Life 200/Milwaukee	7	6	22,320	8	34
Budweiser/G.I. Joe's 200/Portland	6	12	19,800	1	35
Budweiser Cleveland Grand Prix	4	2	39,180	16	51
Molson Indy/Toronto	5	5	34,340	10	61
Marlboro Grand Prix/Meadowlands	10	5	41,340	10	71
Marlboro 500/Michigan	4	2	71,996	16	87
Quaker State 500/Pocono	3	1	92,789	20	107
Escort Radar Warning 200/Mid-Ohio	3	18	14,650	0	107
Briggs & Stratton 200/Elkhart Lake	5	2	39,180	16	123
Bosch Grand Prix/Nazareth	5	12	16,300	1	124
Champion 300km/Laguna Seca	4	4	30,460	12	136
Nissan Indy Challenge/Miami	9	18	15,275	0	136

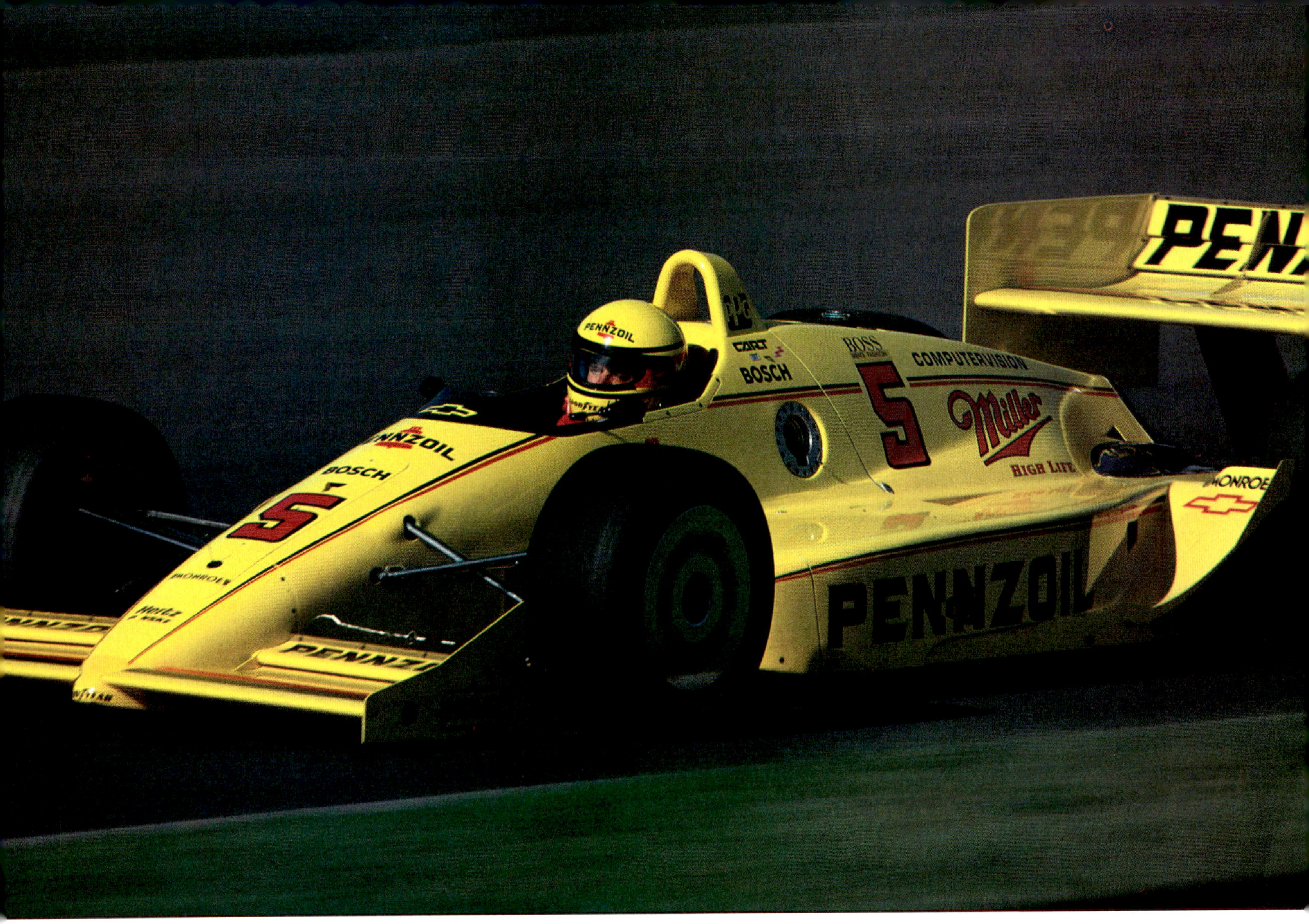

4 Rick Mears

EVENT	START	FINISH	PURSE	POINTS	TOTAL
Checker 200/Phoenix	1	22	$ 18,830	1	1
Toyota Grand Prix of Long Beach	3	8	28,480	5	6
Indianapolis 500	1	1	804,853	21	27
Miller High Life 200/Milwaukee	3	1	47,460	21	48
Budweiser/G.I. Joe's 200/Portland	3	6	30,720	8	56
Budweiser Cleveland Grand Prix	2	23	13,620	0	56
Molson Indy/Toronto	8	6	30,720	8	64
Marlboro Grand Prix/Meadowlands	5	3	54,500	14	78
Marlboro 500/Michigan	1	13	25,456	2	80
Quaker State 500/Pocono	1	23	25,963	1	81
Escort Radar Warning 200/Mid-Ohio	5	3	34,500	14	95
Briggs & Stratton 200/Elkhart Lake	2	12	16,050	1	96
Bosch Grand Prix/Nazareth	2	7	20,600	7	103
Champion 300km/Laguna Seca	7	5	26,840	10	113
Nissan Indy Challenge/Miami	4	2	50,880	16	129

FOR SAFETY'S SAKE...

RAIN-X® dramatically improves wet weather visibility. It extends and expands your field of vision; lets you see clearly with and without wipers! RAIN-X® covers windshields, side and rear windows, mirrors and lights with an invisible shield that disperses rain, sleet and snow on contact – shrugs off bugs, ice, frost, salt, mud and grime to make cleaning a snap. Whatever the weather, whatever you drive – use RAIN-X® for increased all-around visibility, safety and driving comfort.

"Don't Drive Without It!"

Mario Andretti

Available at leading automotive outlets!

5 MARIO ANDRETTI

PPG INDY CAR WORLD SERIES

EVENT	START	FINISH	PURSE	POINTS	TOTAL
Checker 200/Phoenix	3	1	$ 38,460	21	21
Toyota Grand Prix of Long Beach	2	15	20,240	0	21
Indianapolis 500	4	20	130,828	0	21
Miller High Life 200/Milwaukee	2	17	14,580	0	21
Budweiser/G.I. Joe's 200/Portland	5	5	33,840	10	31
Budweiser Cleveland Grand Prix	3	1	45,660	20	51
Molson Indy/Toronto	2	25	15,120	0	51
Marlboro Grand Prix/Meadowlands	2	2	71,880	16	67
Marlboro 500/Michigan	3	12	21,083	1	68
Quaker State 500/Pocono	5	17	16,780	0	68
Escort Radar Warning 200/Mid-Ohio	4	2	43,880	16	84
Briggs & Stratton 200/Elkhart Lake	6	3	29,500	14	98
Bosch Grand Prix/Nazareth	3	3	30,500	14	112
Champion 300km/Laguna Seca	2	3	34,500	14	126
Nissan Indy Challenge/Miami	2	15	17,240	0	126

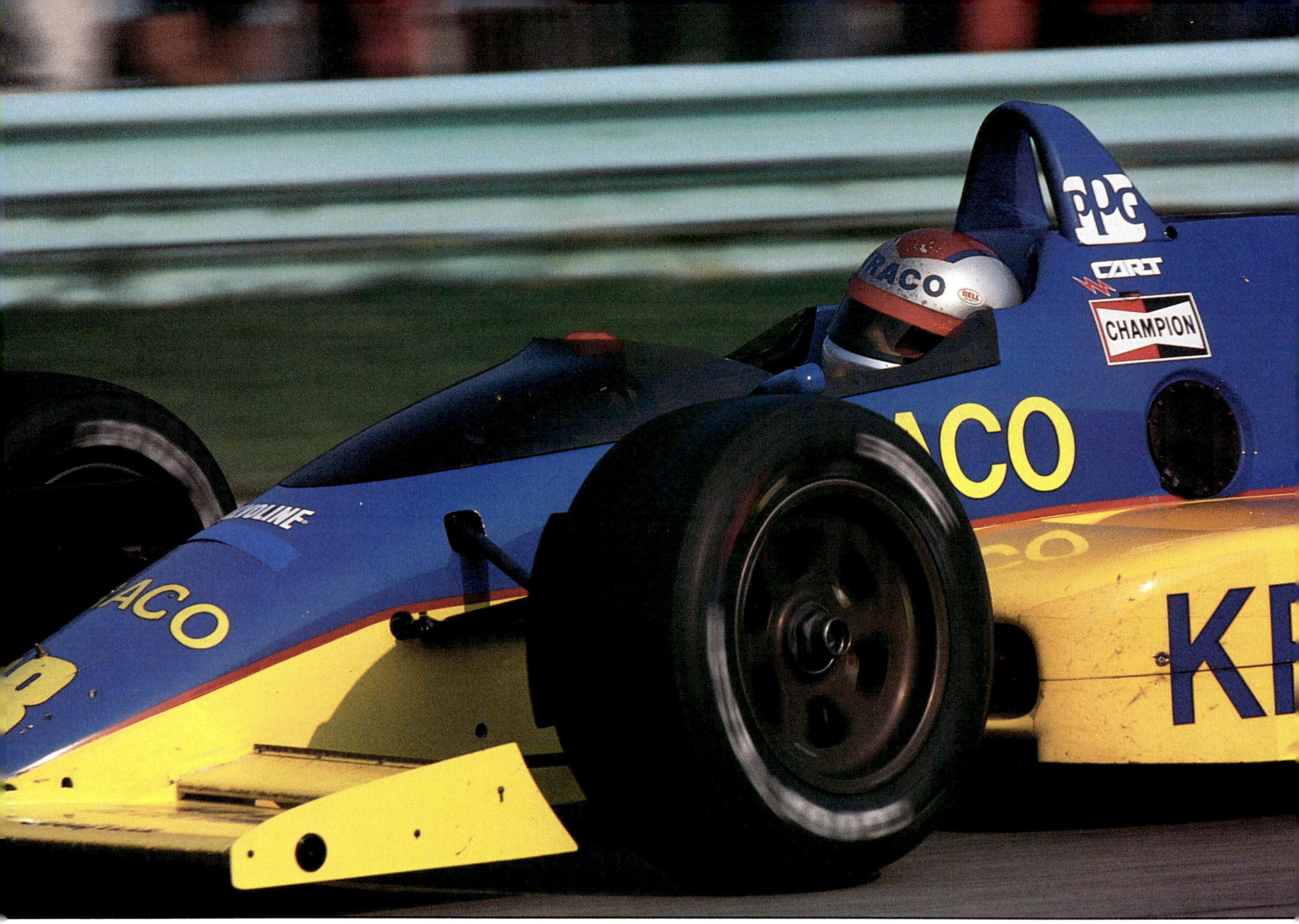

6 MICHAEL ANDRETTI

PPG INDY CAR WORLD SERIES

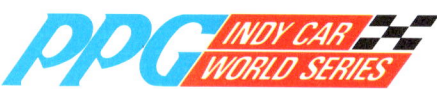

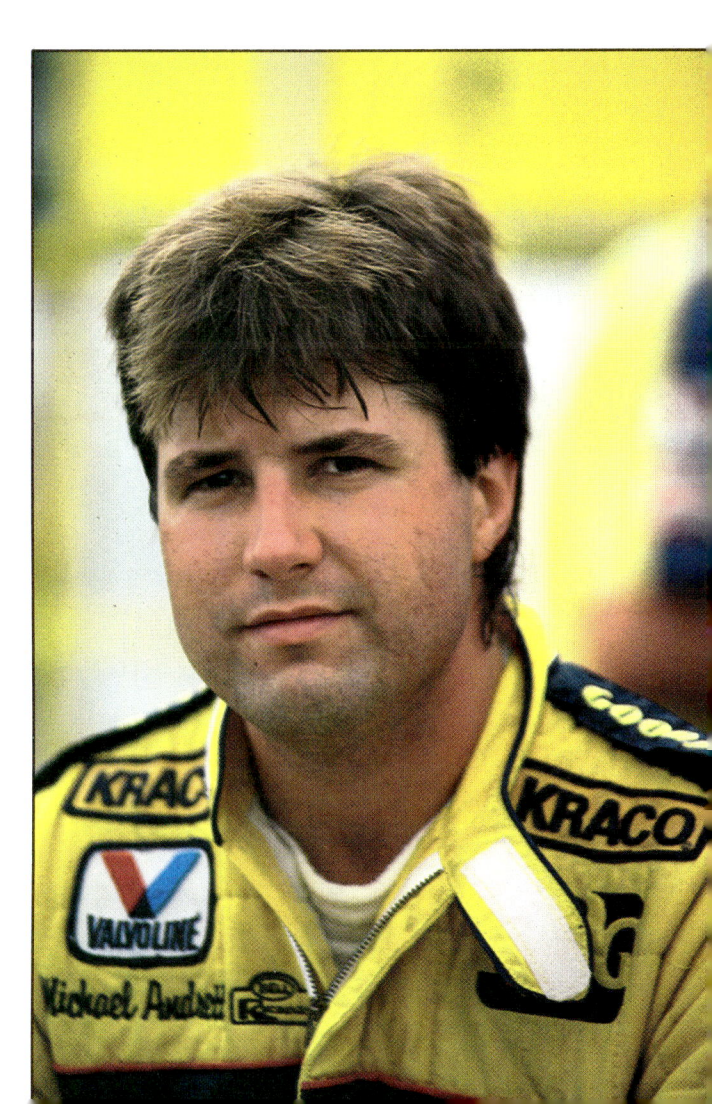

EVENT	START	FINISH	PURSE	POINTS	TOTAL
Checker 200/Phoenix	10	3	$ 26,450	14	14
Toyota Grand Prix of Long Beach	5	7	32,600	6	20
Indianapolis 500	10	4	192,753	12	32
Miller High Life 200/Milwaukee	1	7	25,600	7	39
Budweiser/G.I. Joe's 200/Portland	8	11	20,424	2	41
Budweiser Cleveland Grand Prix	7	14	15,240	0	41
Molson Indy/Toronto	6	3	45,450	14	55
Marlboro Grand Prix/Meadowlands	9	6	36,720	8	63
Marlboro 500/Michigan	14	3	46,226	14	77
Quaker State 500/Pocono	12	25	15,729	0	77
Escort Radar Warning 200/Mid-Ohio	7	26	14,120	0	77
Briggs & Stratton 200/Elkhart Lake	8	5	23,840	10	87
Bosch Grand Prix/Nazareth	8	2	40,580	16	103
Champion 300km/Laguna Seca	5	2	46,180	16	119
Nissan Indy Challenge/Miami	3	17	15,275	0	119

7 Emerson Fittipaldi

PPG INDY CAR WORLD SERIES

EVENT	START	FINISH	PURSE	POINTS	TOTAL
Checker 200/Phoenix	14	21	$ 13,830	0	0
Toyota Grand Prix of Long Beach	7	16	18,180	0	0
Indianapolis 500	8	2	335,103	16	16
Miller High Life 200/Milwaukee	10	3	34,000	14	30
Budweiser/G.I. Joe's 200/Portland	7	3	48,000	14	44
Budweiser Cleveland Grand Prix	6	19	17,525	0	44
Molson Indy/Toronto	4	4	40,460	12	56
Marlboro Grand Prix/Meadowlands	1	14	28,740	2	58
Marlboro 500/Michigan	7	19	21,447	0	58
Quaker State 500/Pocono	8	21	19,696	0	58
Escort Radar Warning 200/Mid-Ohio	6	1	58,160	21	79
Briggs & Stratton 200/Elkhart Lake	4	1	49,160	21	100
Bosch Grand Prix/Nazareth	4	8	22,380	5	105
Champion 300km/Laguna Seca	6	16	18,680	0	105
Nissan Indy Challenge/Miami	6	20	18,775	0	105

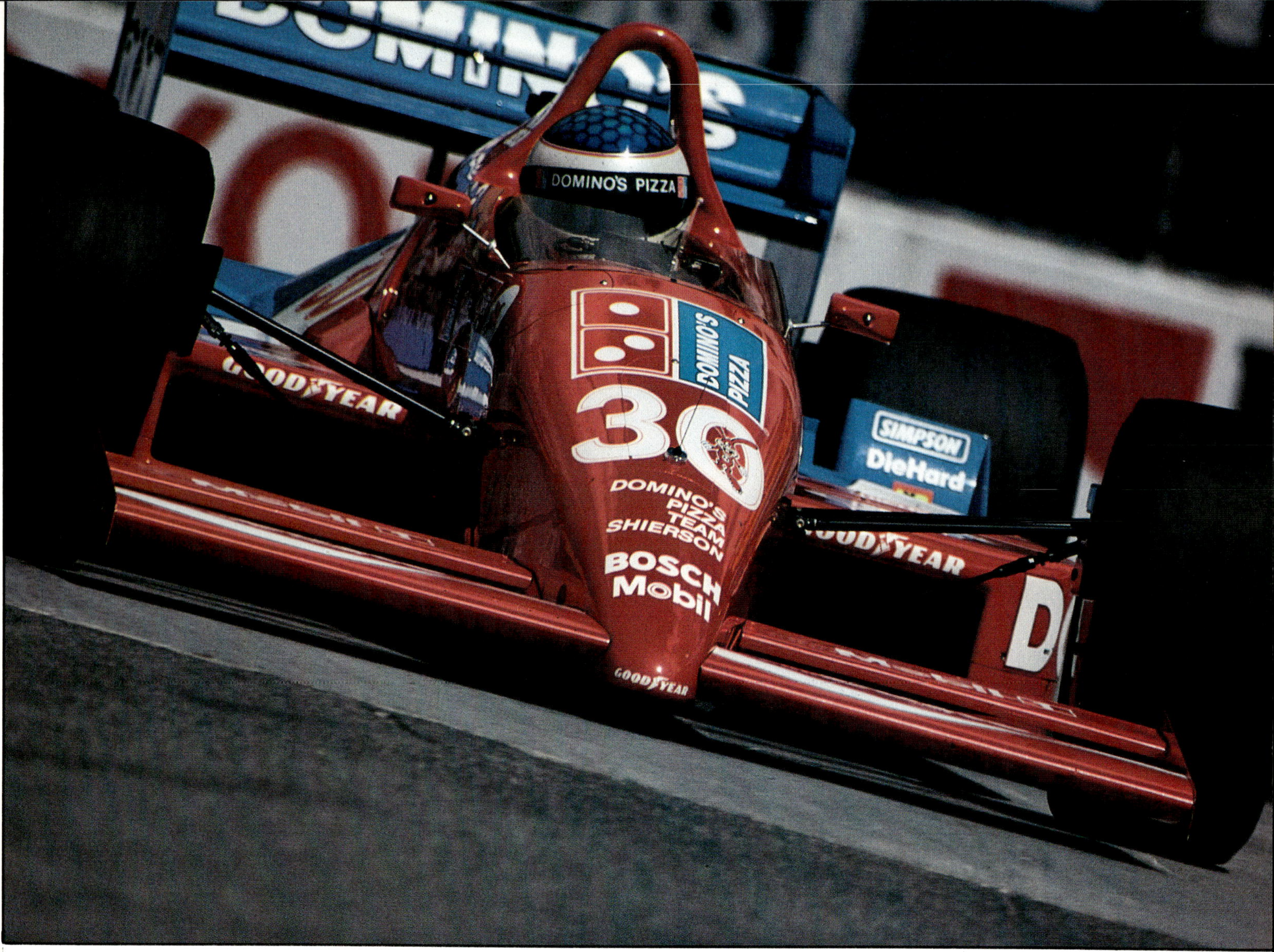

8 Raul Boesel

PPG INDY CAR WORLD SERIES

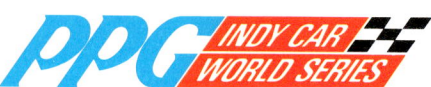

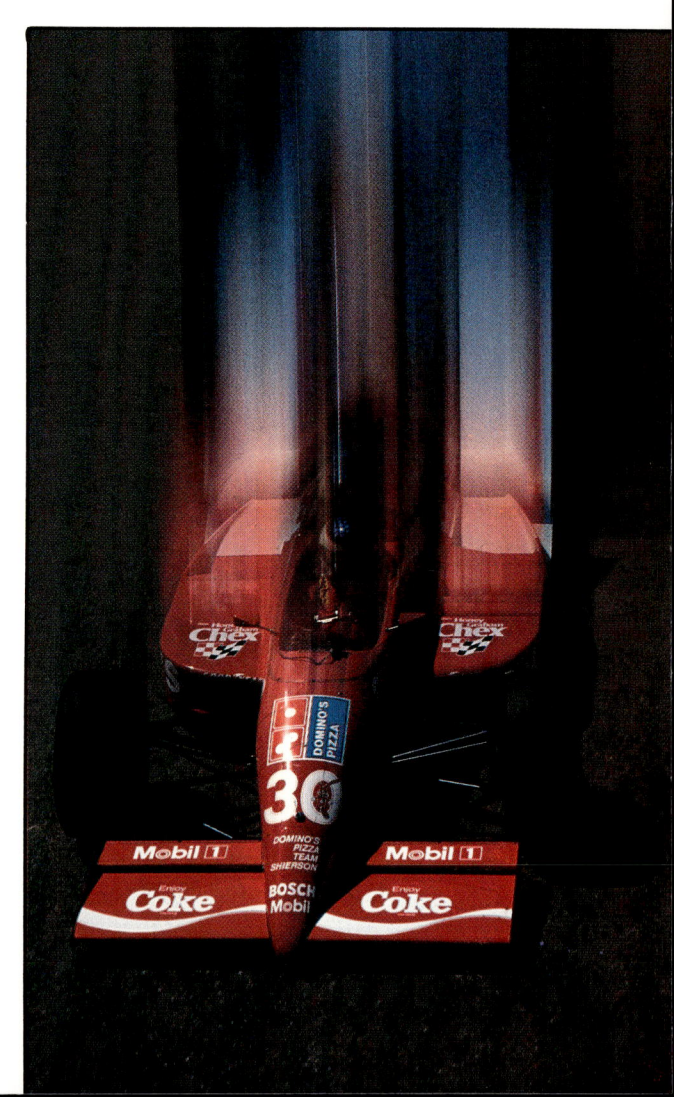

EVENT	START	FINISH	PURSE	POINTS	TOTAL
Checker 200/Phoenix	13	5	$ 20,540	10	10
Toyota Grand Prix of Long Beach	6	4	45,710	12	22
Indianapolis 500	20	7	148,403	6	28
Miller High Life 200/Milwaukee	6	4	26,510	12	40
Budweiser/G.I. Joe's 200/Portland	16	20	15,120	0	40
Budweiser Cleveland Grand Prix	11	5	23,340	10	50
Molson Indy/Toronto	9	8	24,480	5	55
Marlboro Grand Prix/Meadowlands	7	9	24,360	4	59
Marlboro 500/Michigan	10	11	21,710	2	61
Quaker State 500/Pocono	9	5	24,139	10	71
Escort Radar Warning 200/Mid-Ohio	26	6	19,720	8	79
Briggs & Stratton 200/Elkhart Lake	11	14	15,240	0	79
Bosch Grand Prix/Nazareth	7	5	24,040	10	89
Champion 300km/Laguna Seca	11	21	14,120	0	89
Nissan Indy Challenge/Miami	8	22	14,620	0	89

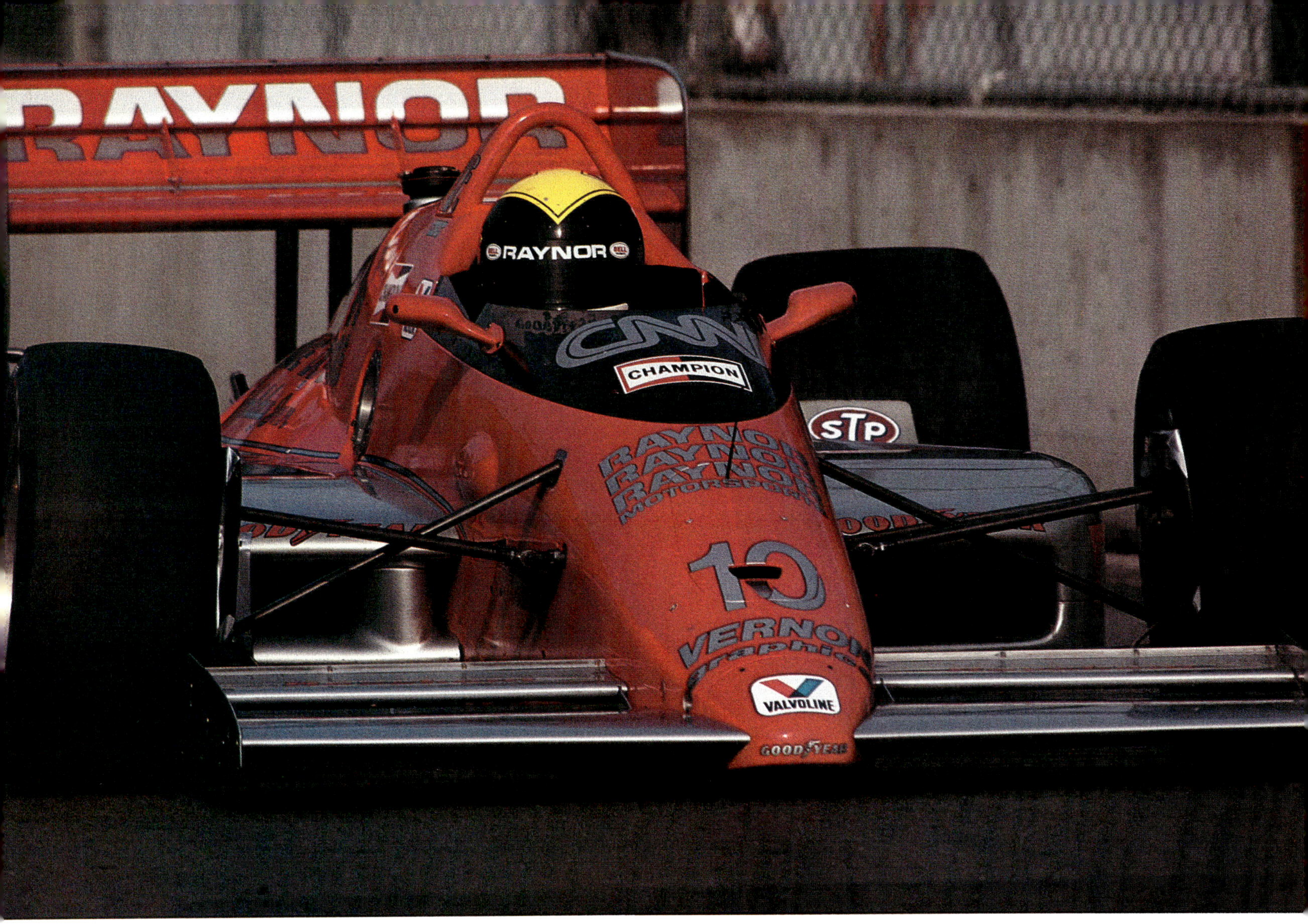

9 DEREK DALY

PPG INDY CAR WORLD SERIES

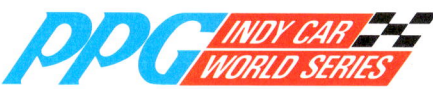

EVENT	START	FINISH	PURSE	POINTS	TOTAL
Checker 200/Phoenix	13	15	$ 15,050	0	0
Toyota Grand Prix of Long Beach	14	5	41,340	10	10
Indianapolis 500	9	29	97,503	0	10
Miller High Life 200/Milwaukee	8	11	16,644	2	12
Budweiser/G.I. Joe's 200/Portland	10	19	15,900	0	12
Budweiser Cleveland Grand Prix	9	6	21,720	8	20
Molson Indy/Toronto	7	23	15,120	0	20
Marlboro Grand Prix/Meadowlands	12	24	16,120	0	20
Marlboro 500/Michigan	8	16	18,574	0	20
Quaker State 500/Pocono	10	4	29,143	12	32
Escort Radar Warning 200/Mid-Ohio	10	9	18,360	4	36
Briggs & Stratton 200/Elkhart Lake	10	6	21,720	8	44
Bosch Grand Prix/Nazareth	10	9	16,816	3	47
Champion 300km/Laguna Seca	9	7	22,600	6	53
Nissan Indy Challenge/Miami	10	23	14,620	0	53

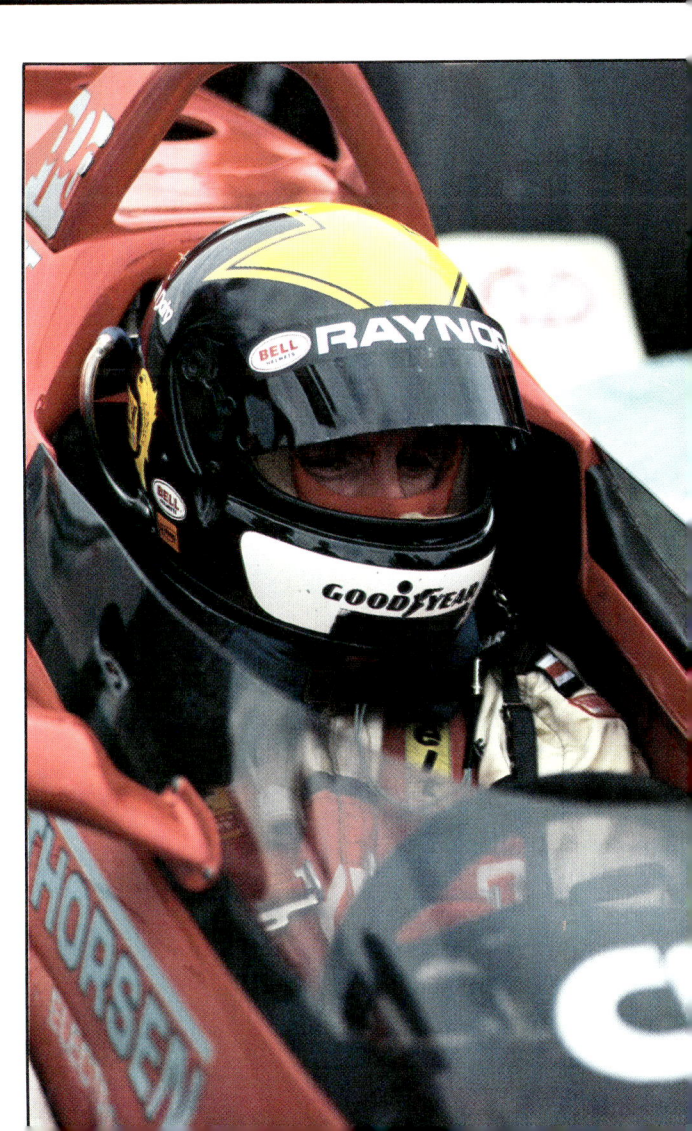

Driver Derek Daly and his
Raynor Garage Door Lola

Every Indy Car Parks Behind a Raynor Door.

Since the end of WWI, when Dusenbergs, Sunbeams, Mercedes and Studebakers were lapping the oval at the Indianapolis Motor Speedway, racing cars have been housed in an area that became a legend known as "Gasoline Alley." To keep pace with the changing world of auto racing, Indy's management decided to raze the wooden cubicles that comprised this famous landmark and replace them with the most efficient, practical and modern racing car garage complex ever conceived.

Because the folks at Indy live, eat and breathe performance, it was only fitting that they'd insist on a high performance door for their 110 individual garages. That's why they specified Raynor Rolling Steel Service doors.

Now your door needs may not be exactly the same as those at the Indianapolis Motor Speedway, but you probably want garage doors that meet their same high set of standards. If that's the case, just call the number they did: **1-800-545-0455,** or look in the Yellow Pages under "Doors."

RAYNOR GARAGE DOORS
Residential, Commercial, Industrial

How to beat the traffic home.

Ever since Porsche's first official win on July 11, 1948 at Innsbruck, Austria, Porsches have taken more checkered flags in sprint, endurance and rally racing than any other car.

Which is why a day at the races can be such an inspiring event for the spectator.

So inspiring in fact, that, for some of you, the thought of having to drive home in whatever it was you arrived in could be enough to make you plan a trip to your local Porsche dealer.

Tomorrow.

If not sooner.

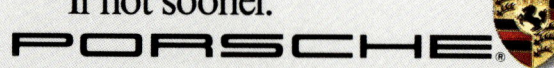

The Porsche experience begins with your authorized Porsche dealer.

©1986 Porsche Cars North America, Inc.

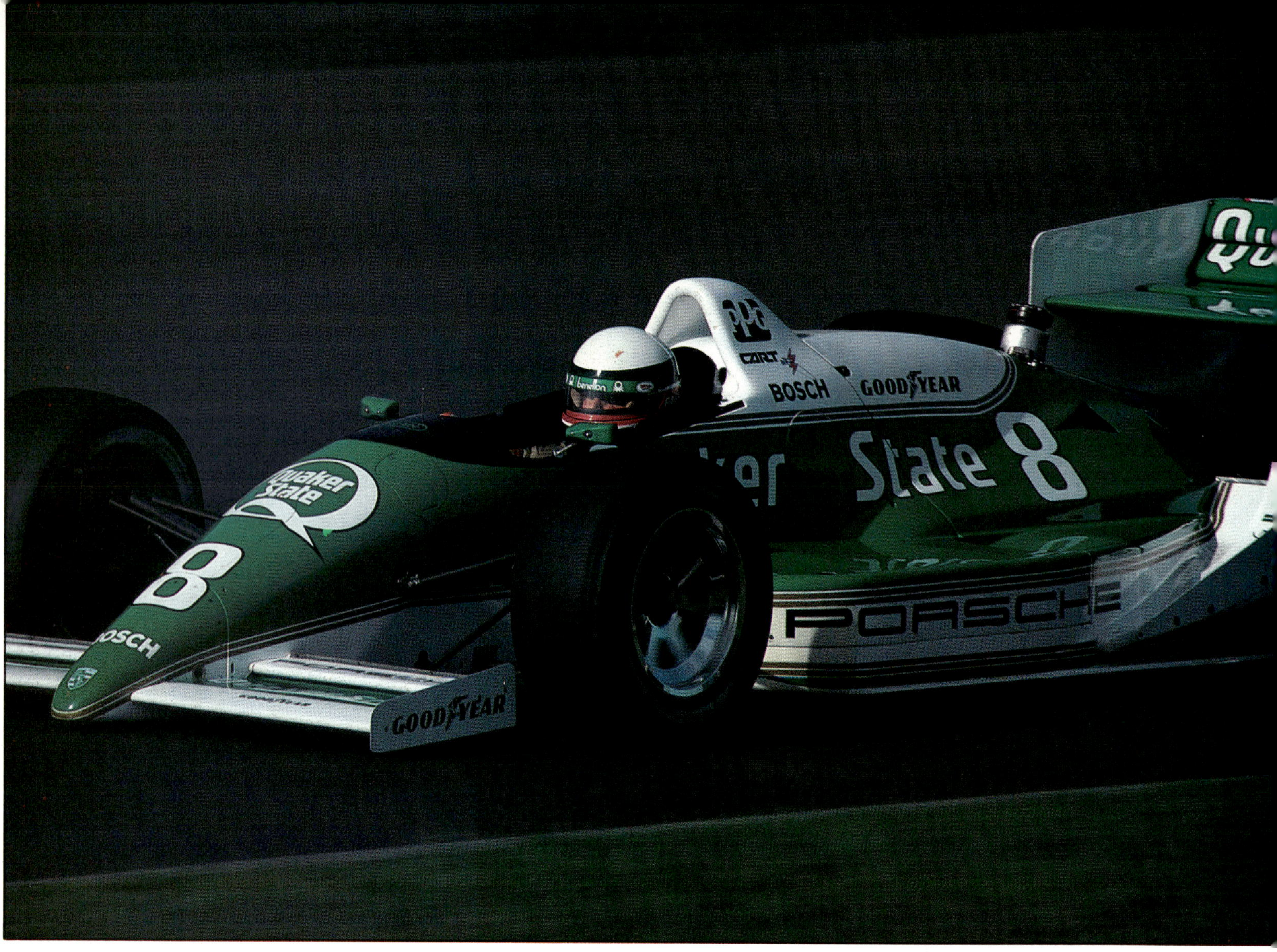

10 Teo Fabi

EVENT	START	FINISH	PURSE	POINTS	TOTAL
Checker 200/Phoenix	9	7	$ 11,100	6	6
Toyota Grand Prix of Long Beach	12	24	9,120	0	6
Indianapolis 500	17	28	101,878	0	6
Miller High Life 200/Milwaukee	16	9	10,160	4	10
Budweiser/G.I. Joe's 200/Portland	9	7	20,600	6	16
Budweiser Cleveland Grand Prix	16	24	6,620	0	16
Molson Indy/Toronto	10	10	13,736	3	19
Marlboro Grand Prix/Meadowlands	3	18	10,150	0	19
Marlboro 500/Michigan	12	25	10,006	0	19
Quaker State 500/Pocono	25	24	8,846	0	19
Escort Radar Warning 200/Mid-Ohio	11	8	13,480	5	24
Briggs & Stratton 200/Elkhart Lake	13	8	11,480	5	29
Bosch Grand Prix/Nazareth	12	4	19,510	12	41
Champion 300km/Laguna Seca	8	10	10,936	3	44
Nissan Indy Challenge/Miami	7	21	7,620	0	44

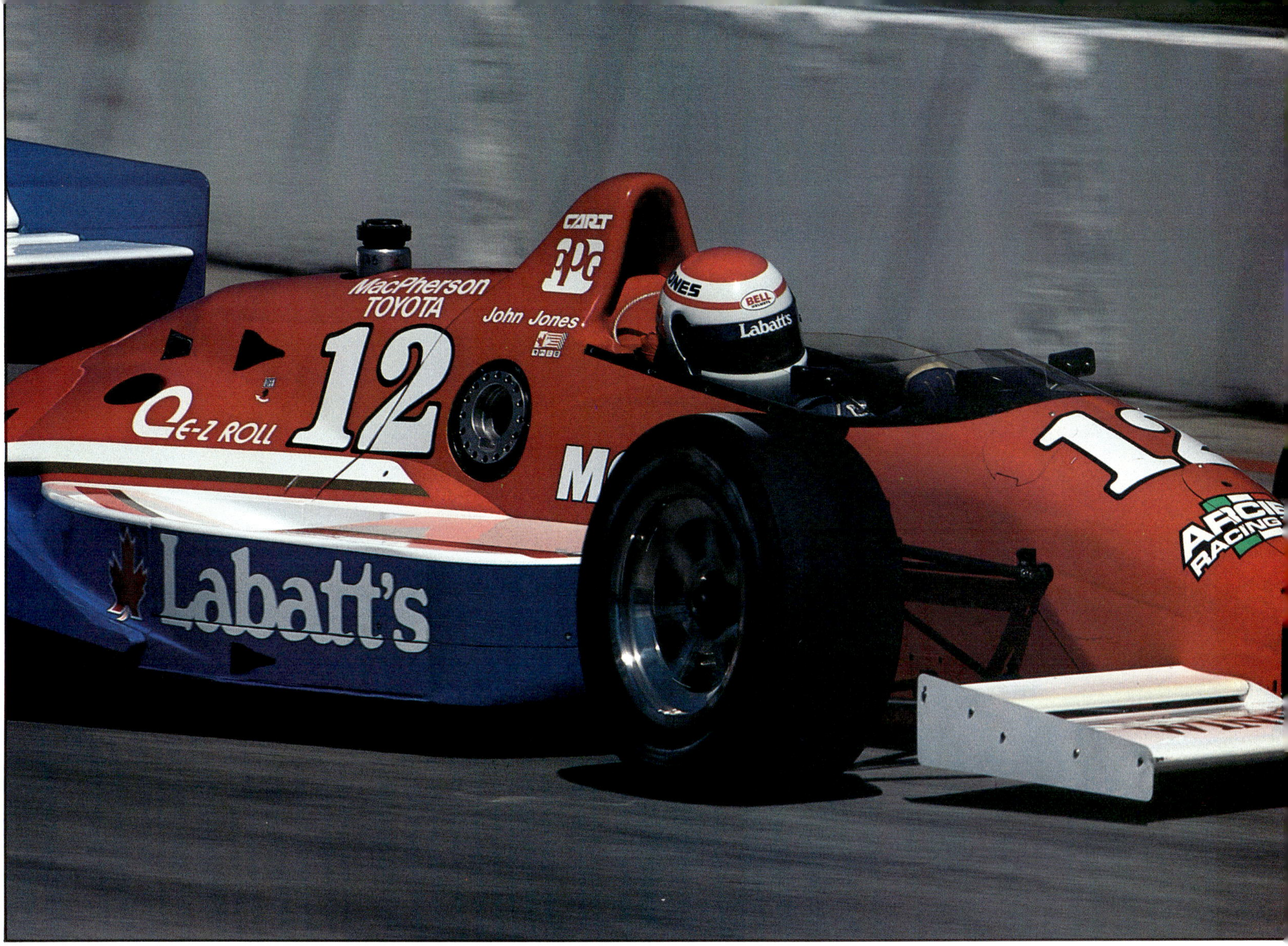

11 JOHN JONES

PPG INDY CAR WORLD SERIES

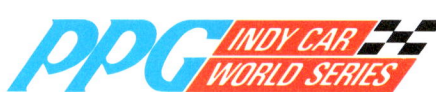

EVENT	START	FINISH	PURSE	POINTS	TOTAL
Checker 200/Phoenix	19	20	$ 13,830	0	0
Toyota Grand Prix of Long Beach	21	12	22,300	1	1
Indianapolis 500	DNS			0	1
Miller High Life 200/Milwaukee	17	14	15,440	0	1
Budweiser/G.I. Joe's 200/Portland	15	8	24,480	5	6
Budweiser Cleveland Grand Prix	14	7	20,100	6	12
Molson Indy/Toronto	13	7	27,600	6	18
Marlboro Grand Prix/Meadowlands	19	7	32,600	6	24
Marlboro 500/Michigan	26	8	23,592	5	29
Quaker State 500/Pocono	24	8	20,635	5	34
Escort Radar Warning 200/Mid-Ohio	13	7	22,600	6	40
Briggs & Stratton 200/Elkhart Lake	15	13	16,050	0	40
Bosch Grand Prix/Nazareth	16	11	16,644	2	42
Champion 300km/Laguna Seca	15	11	17,724	2	44
Nissan Indy Challenge/Miami	14	16	15,930	0	44

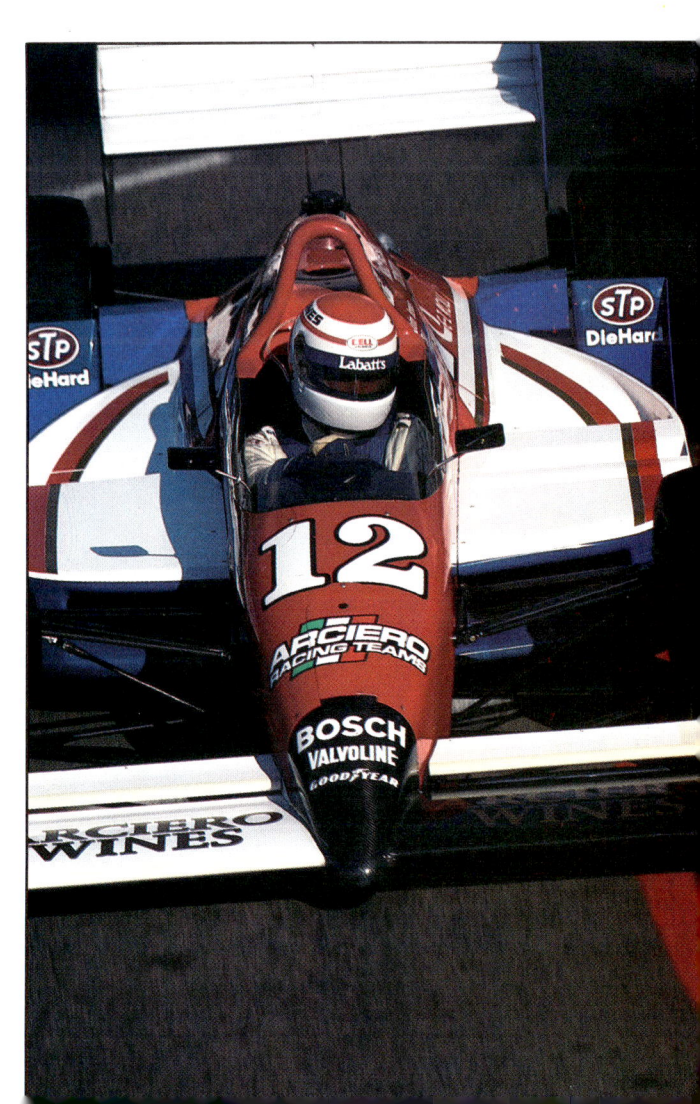

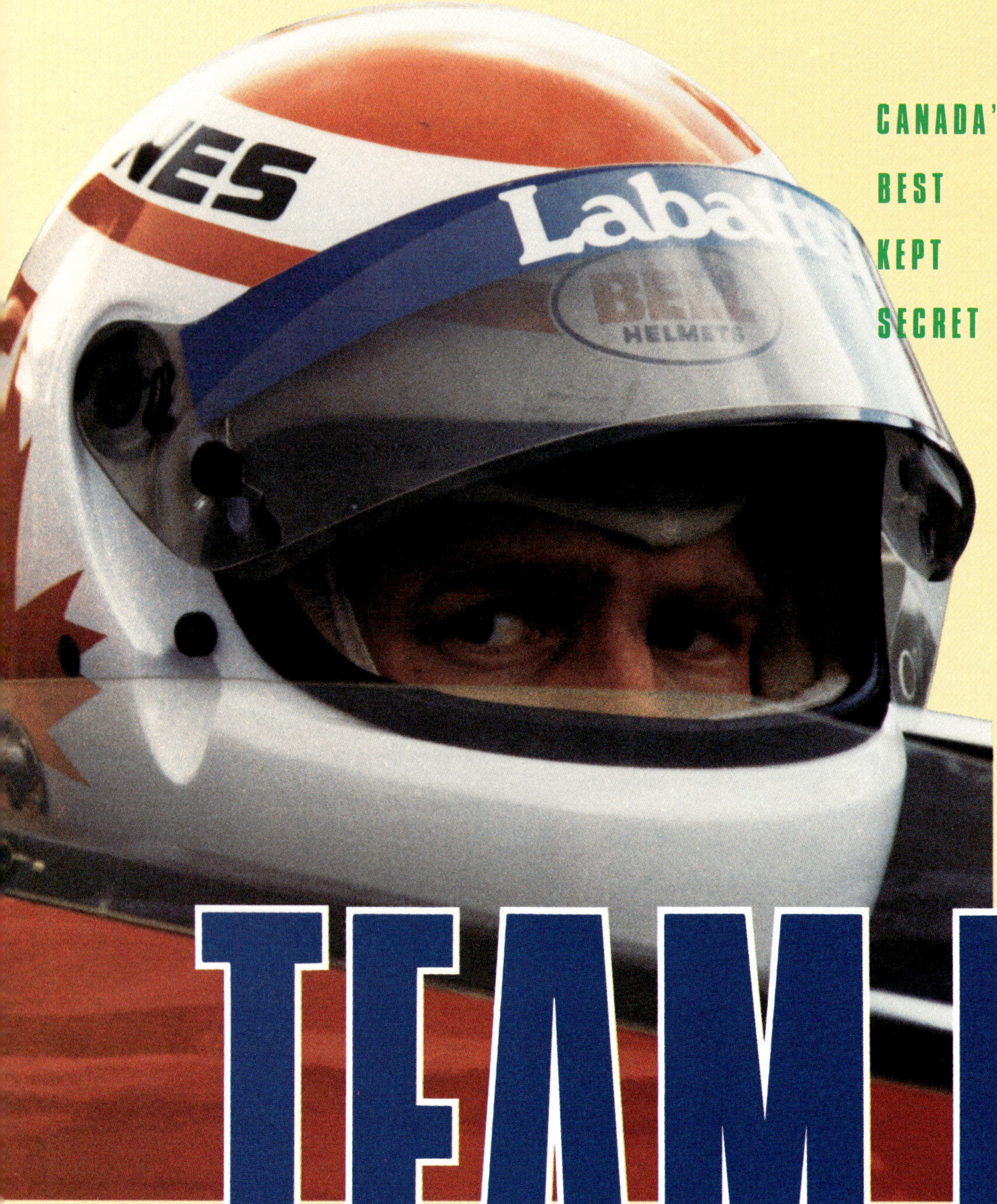

CANADA'S
BEST
KEPT
SECRET

AND
CANADA'S
BEST

TEAM UP

Canada's best kept secret is out! For the past 2 years Labatt's Blue has sponsored John Jones and is proud of John's CART Rookie of the Year title. Labatt's looks forward to his continuing success and a time when the best kept secret is simply known as the best.

12 ROBERTO GUERRERO

EVENT	START	FINISH	PURSE	POINTS	TOTAL
Checker 200/Phoenix	2	2	$ 32,780	16	16
Toyota Grand Prix of Long Beach	10	19	17,150	0	16
Indianapolis 500	12	32	100,828	0	16
Miller High Life 200/Milwaukee	DNS		7,000	0	16
Budweiser/G.I. Joe's 200/Portland	23	14	18,240	0	16
Budweiser Cleveland Grand Prix	15	20	14,025	0	16
Molson Indy/Toronto	DNS			0	16
Marlboro Grand Prix/Meadowlands	DNS			0	16
Marlboro 500/Michigan	16	20	17,790	0	16
Quaker State 500/Pocono	16	3	37,369	14	30
Escort Radar Warning 200/Mid-Ohio	14	11	17,724	2	32
Briggs & Stratton 200/Elkhart Lake	12	22	13,620	0	32
Bosch Grand Prix/Nazareth	11	6	22,320	8	40
Champion 300km/Laguna Seca	13	14	16,240	0	40
Nissan Indy Challenge/Miami	19	26	14,620	0	40

IAM
Keeping America On the Right Track

American genius is alive and well. Building cars that top 215 miles-per-hour. Fighter jets that dance and soar at twice the speed of sound. Planes that move millions of passengers each year, in safety and quiet.

The International Association of Machinists and Aerospace Workers (IAM) is proud that our 800,000 members produce the most advanced products on earth—from jet engines and rockets to nuclear submarines and space stations.

The IAM is proud that our skills and hard work have helped make America—and Indy Car Racing—great.

The IAM leads the fight to keep these skills, jobs and technologies in America—to keep America on the right track as we move into the 21st Century.

International Association of Machinists and Aerospace Workers

1300 Connecticut Avenue, N.W., Washington DC 20036
William W. Winpisinger, International President

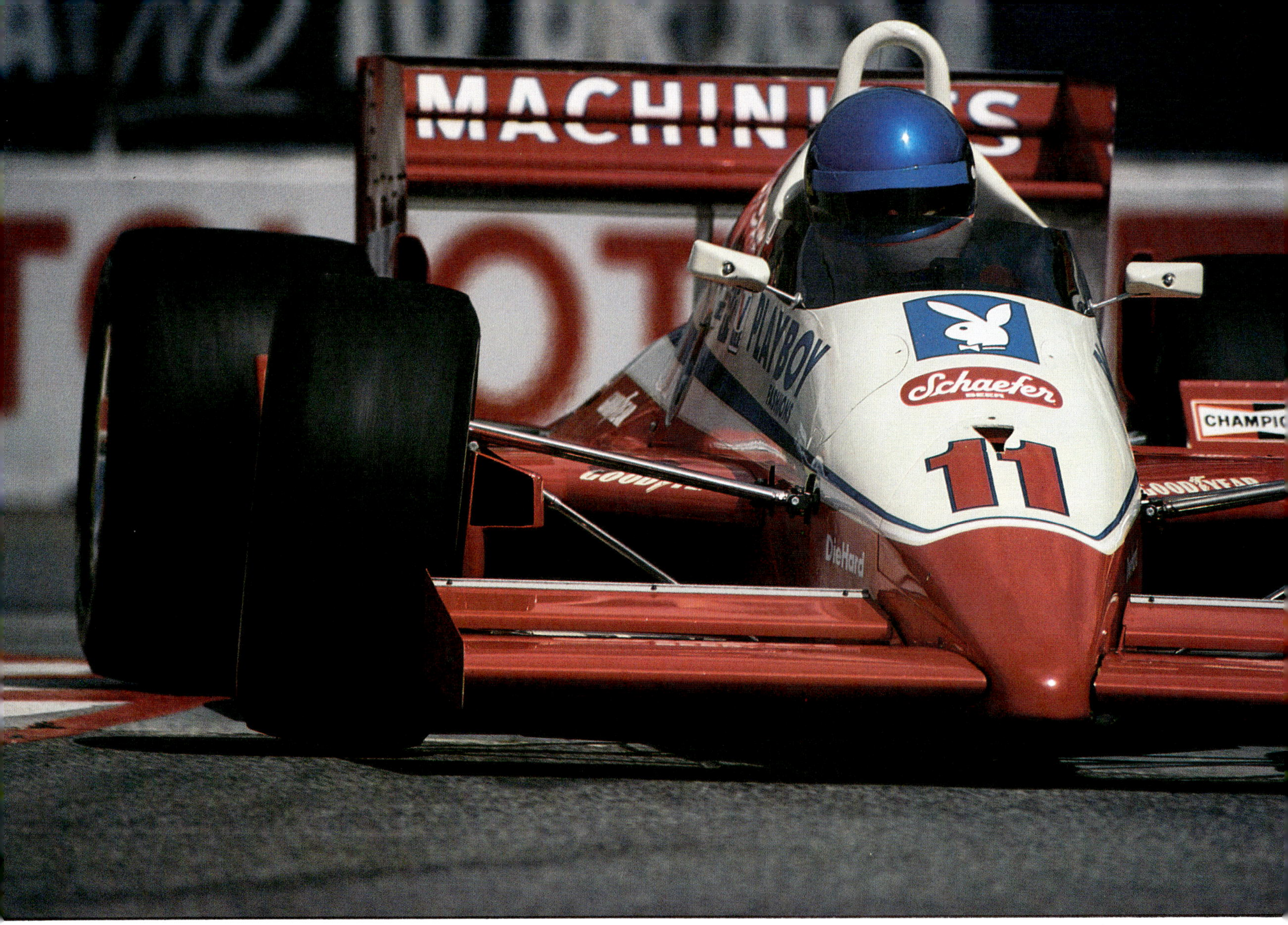

13 Kevin Cogan

EVENT	START	FINISH	PURSE	POINTS	TOTAL
Checker 200/Phoenix	20	8	$ 16,880	5	5
Toyota Grand Prix of Long Beach	18	3	55,450	14	19
Indianapolis 500	13	11	141,078	2	21
Miller High Life 200/Milwaukee	19	22	14,580	0	21
Budweiser/G.I. Joe's 200/Portland	14	20	15,900	0	21
Budweiser Cleveland Grand Prix	13	10	16,536	3	24
Molson Indy/Toronto	15	24	15,120	0	24
Marlboro Grand Prix/Meadowlands	DNS			0	24
Marlboro 500/Michigan	DNS			0	24
Quaker State 500/Pocono	DNS			0	24
Escort Radar Warning 200/Mid-Ohio	DNS			0	24
Briggs & Stratton 200/Elkhart Lake	7	24	13,620	0	24
Bosch Grand Prix/Nazareth	15	15	15,440	0	24
Champion 300km/Laguna Seca	10	9	18,360	4	28
Nissan Indy Challenge/Miami	13	4	34,460	12	40

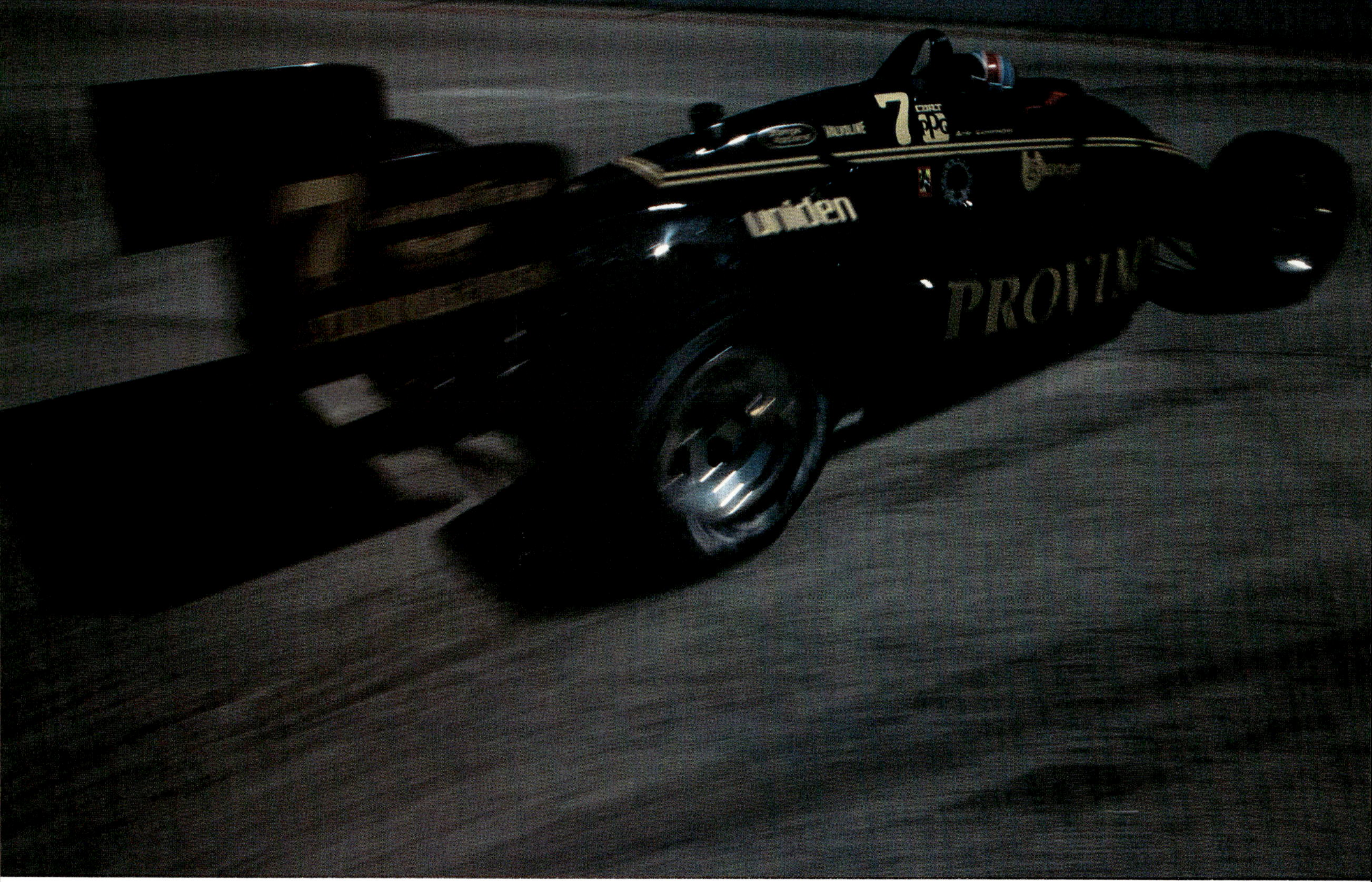

14 Arie Luyendyk

PPG INDY CAR WORLD SERIES

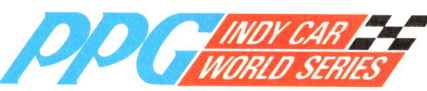

EVENT	START	FINISH	PURSE	POINTS	TOTAL
Checker 200/Phoenix	5	9	$ 15,660	4	4
Toyota Grand Prix of Long Beach	9	10	23,536	3	7
Indianapolis 500	6	10	123,028	3	10
Miller High Life 200/Milwaukee	9	15	15,440	0	10
Budweiser/G.I. Joe's 200/Portland	2	2	60,180	17	27
Budweiser Cleveland Grand Prix	5	18	14,025	0	27
Molson Indy/Toronto	12	20	15,900	0	27
Marlboro Grand Prix/Meadowlands	11	20	17,150	0	27
Marlboro 500/Michigan	11	28	16,536	0	27
Quaker State 500/Pocono	14	26	15,612	0	27
Escort Radar Warning 200/Mid-Ohio	15	25	14,120	0	27
Briggs & Stratton 200/Elkhart Lake	16	19	14,025	0	27
Bosch Grand Prix/Nazareth	13	9	17,160	4	31
Champion 300km/Laguna Seca	12	22	14,120	0	31
Nissan Indy Challenge/Miami	11	14	17,240	0	31

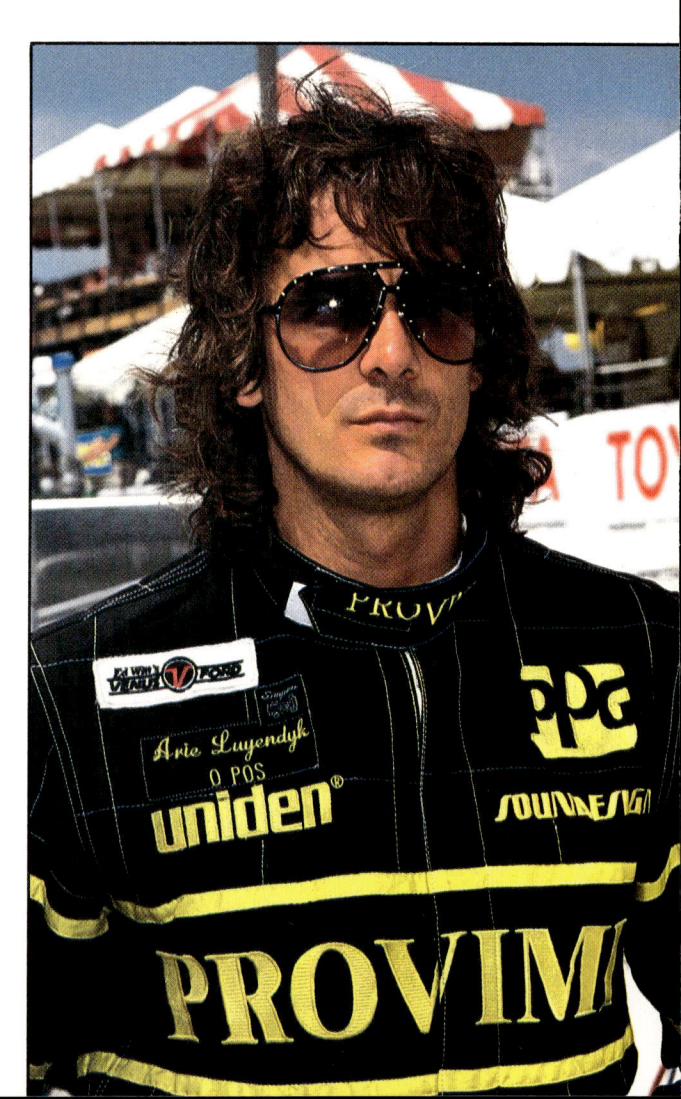

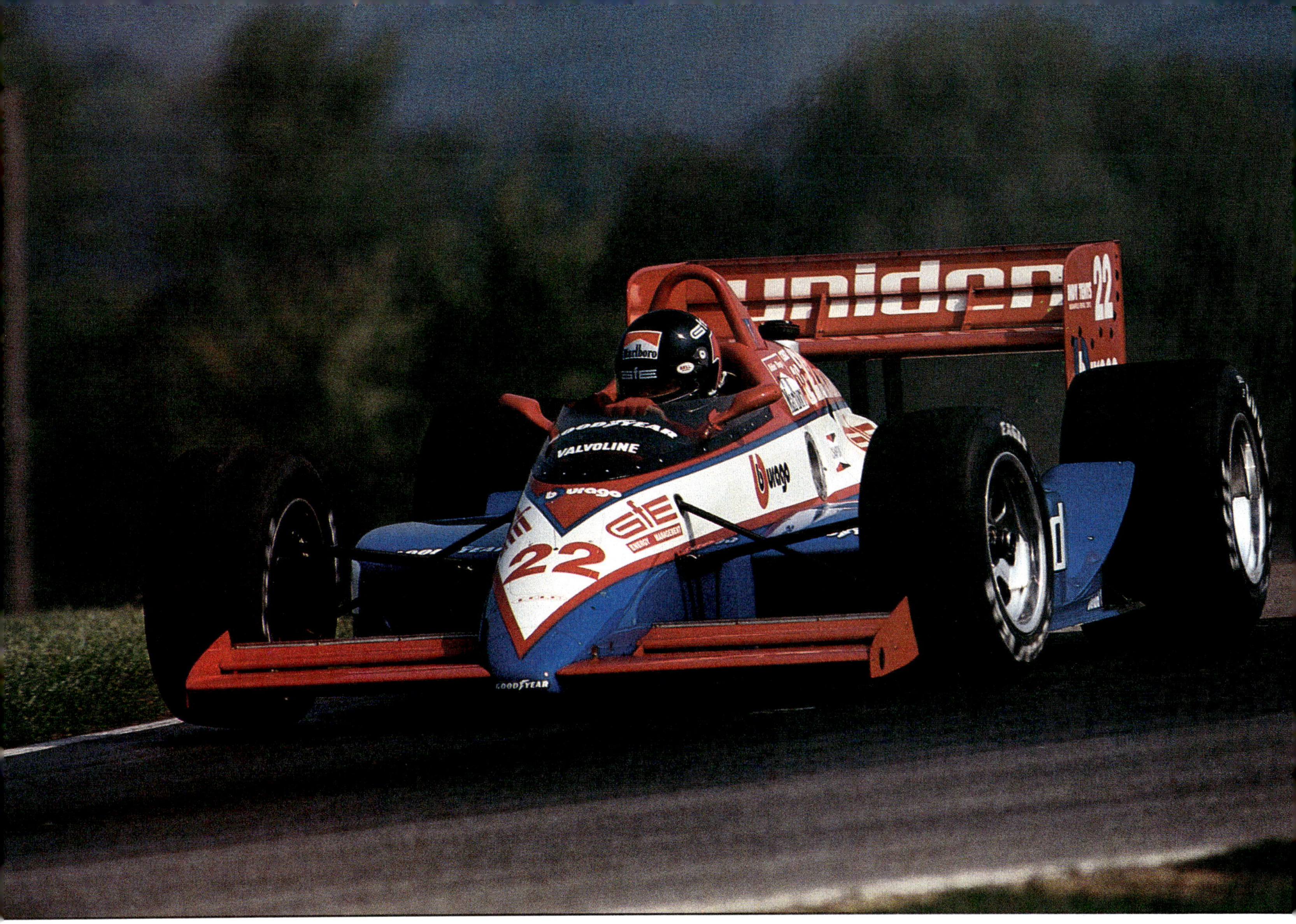

15 DIDIER THEYS

EVENT	START	FINISH	PURSE	POINTS	TOTAL
Checker 200/Phoenix	DNS			0	0
Toyota Grand Prix of Long Beach	DNS			0	0
Indianapolis 500	DNS			0	0
Miller High Life 200/Milwaukee	DNS			0	0
Budweiser/G.I. Joe's 200/Portland	13	10	$ 20,736	3	3
Budweiser Cleveland Grand Prix	8	9	16,860	4	7
Molson Indy/Toronto	11	18	15,900	0	7
Marlboro Grand Prix/Meadowlands	8	21	16,120	0	7
Marlboro 500/Michigan	DNS			0	7
Quaker State 500/Pocono	DNS			0	7
Escort Radar Warning 200/Mid-Ohio	9	10	17,936	3	10
Briggs & Stratton 200/Elkhart Lake	9	23	13,620	0	10
Bosch Grand Prix/Nazareth	DNS			0	10
Champion 300km/Laguna Seca	16	8	20,480	5	15
Nissan Indy Challenge/Miami	12	3	40,450	14	29

IT'S A GILMORE ENTERPRISE THAT MAKES THE DIFFERENCE

If it doesn't measure up, it won't carry our name. More than 20 years in auto racing, including the last 16 with the winningest driver ever, A.J. Foyt, has taught us that it takes more than just good intentions to be the best we can be.

Our name is our reputation and we put it on many different businesses. Included are automotive dealerships; television and radio stations, with two recent additions in Dallas-Ft. Worth (pending FCC approval); ad agencies; industrial farms; insurance companies and commercial real estate developments. We're proud of the Gilmore-Foyt Racing Team and the winning attitude it brings to every competition, regardless of the odds. It's the same commitment we bring to every Gilmore Enterprise.

It's what makes the difference.

Jim Gilmore Enterprises
and
The Gilmore Broadcasting Corporation
202 Michigan Building, KALAMAZOO, MICHIGAN 49007

AUTOMOTIVE • TELEVISION • RADIO • AGRICULTURE • ADVERTISING • REAL ESTATE • AUTO RACING

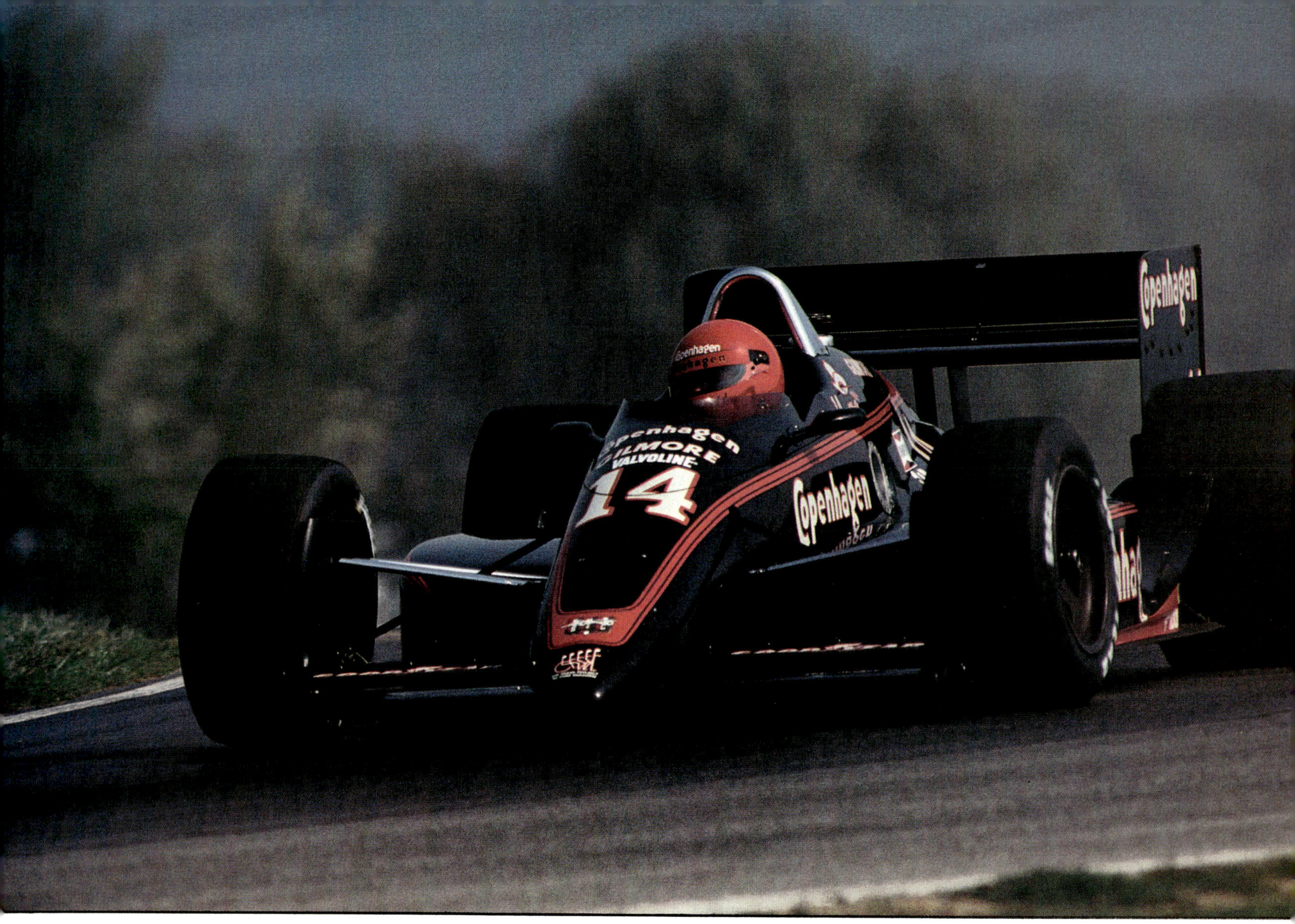

16 A.J. Foyt

EVENT	START	FINISH	PURSE	POINTS	TOTAL
Checker 200/Phoenix	7	4	$ 23,260	12	12
Toyota Grand Prix of Long Beach	23	11	23,124	2	14
Indianapolis 500	22	26	98,853	0	14
Miller High Life 200/Milwaukee	13	5	21,040	10	24
Budweiser/G.I. Joe's 200/Portland	24	15	14,740	0	24
Budweiser Cleveland Grand Prix	21	11	12,874	2	26
Molson Indy/Toronto	19	15	14,740	0	26
Marlboro Grand Prix/Meadowlands	15	17	13,650	0	26
Marlboro 500/Michigan	DNS			0	26
Quaker State 500/Pocono	6	16	13,397	0	26
Escort Radar Warning 200/Mid-Ohio	12	22	10,620	0	26
Briggs & Stratton 200/Elkhart Lake	22	10	13,036	3	29
Bosch Grand Prix/Nazareth	17	17	11,080	0	29
Champion 300km/Laguna Seca	21	24	10,620	0	29
Nissan Indy Challenge/Miami	16	25	11,120	0	29

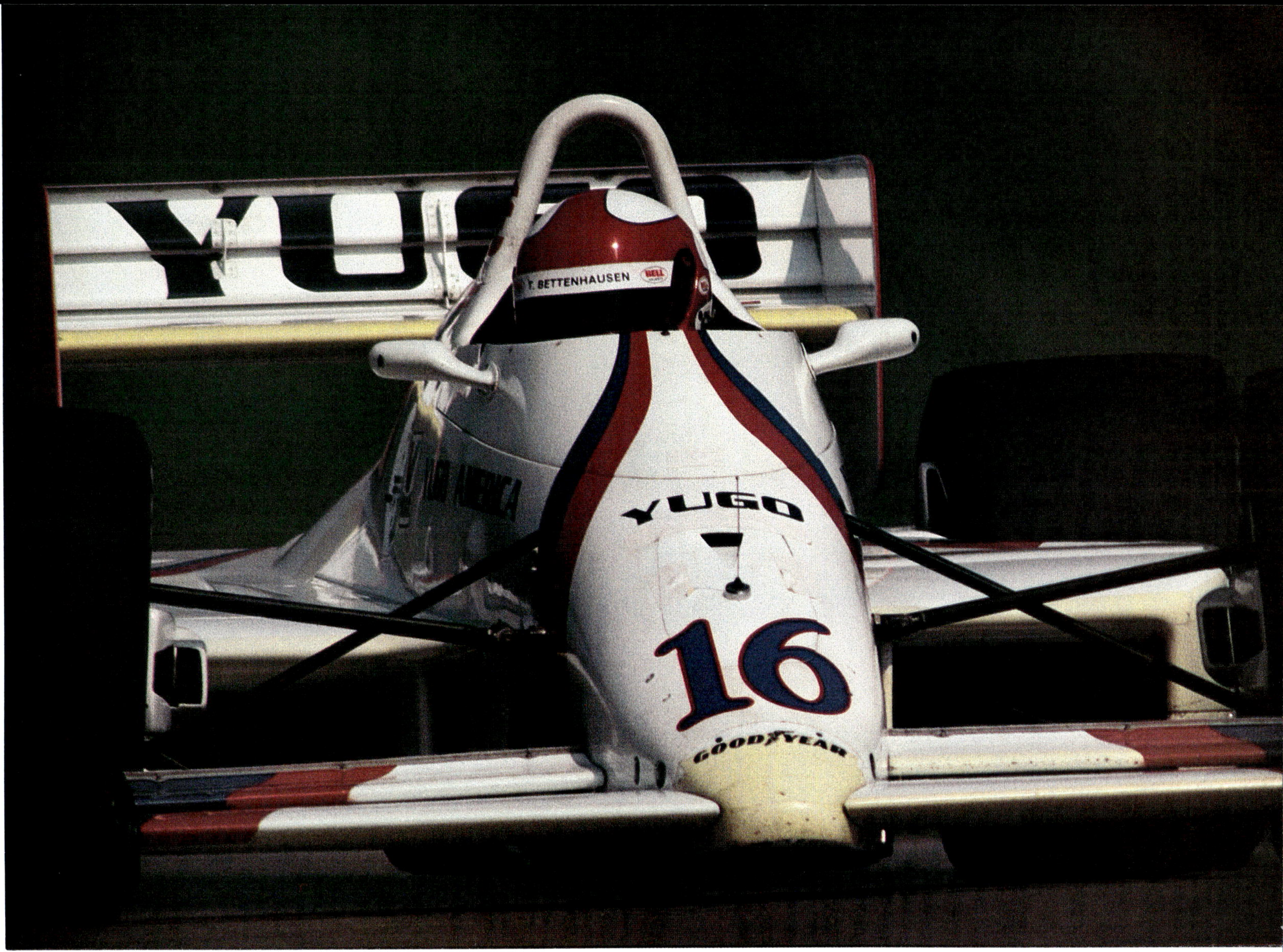

17 Tony Bettenhausen

PPG INDY CAR WORLD SERIES

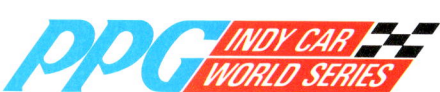

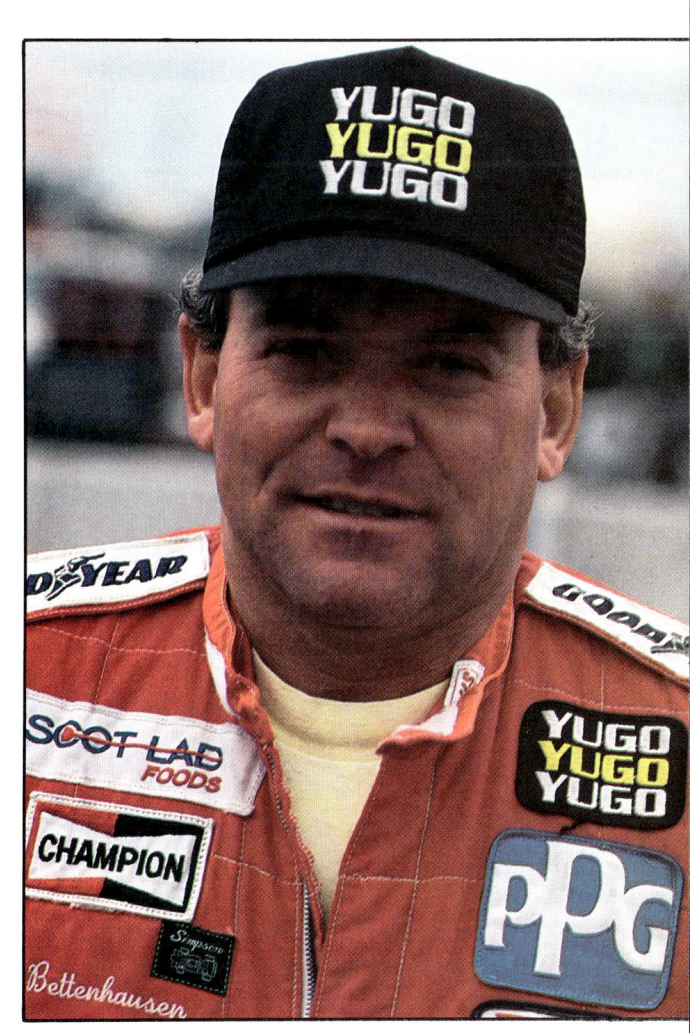

EVENT	START	FINISH	PURSE	POINTS	TOTAL
Checker 200/Phoenix	22	6	$ 19,320	8	8
Toyota Grand Prix of Long Beach	DNS		7,000	0	8
Indianapolis 500	24	33	95,753	0	8
Miller High Life 200/Milwaukee	21	19	11,080	0	8
Budweiser/G.I. Joe's 200/Portland	DNS			0	8
Budweiser Cleveland Grand Prix	22	15	11,740	0	8
Molson Indy/Toronto	23	17	12,400	0	8
Marlboro Grand Prix/Meadowlands	24	8	24,980	5	13
Marlboro 500/Michigan	18	4	31,000	12	25
Quaker State 500/Pocono	15	15	13,864	0	25
Escort Radar Warning 200/Mid-Ohio	23	16	11,680	0	25
Briggs & Stratton 200/Elkhart Lake	17	16	10,930	0	25
Bosch Grand Prix/Nazareth	19	13	12,800	0	25
Champion 300km/Laguna Seca	25	26	5,620	0	25
Nissan Indy Challenge/Miami	DNS			0	25

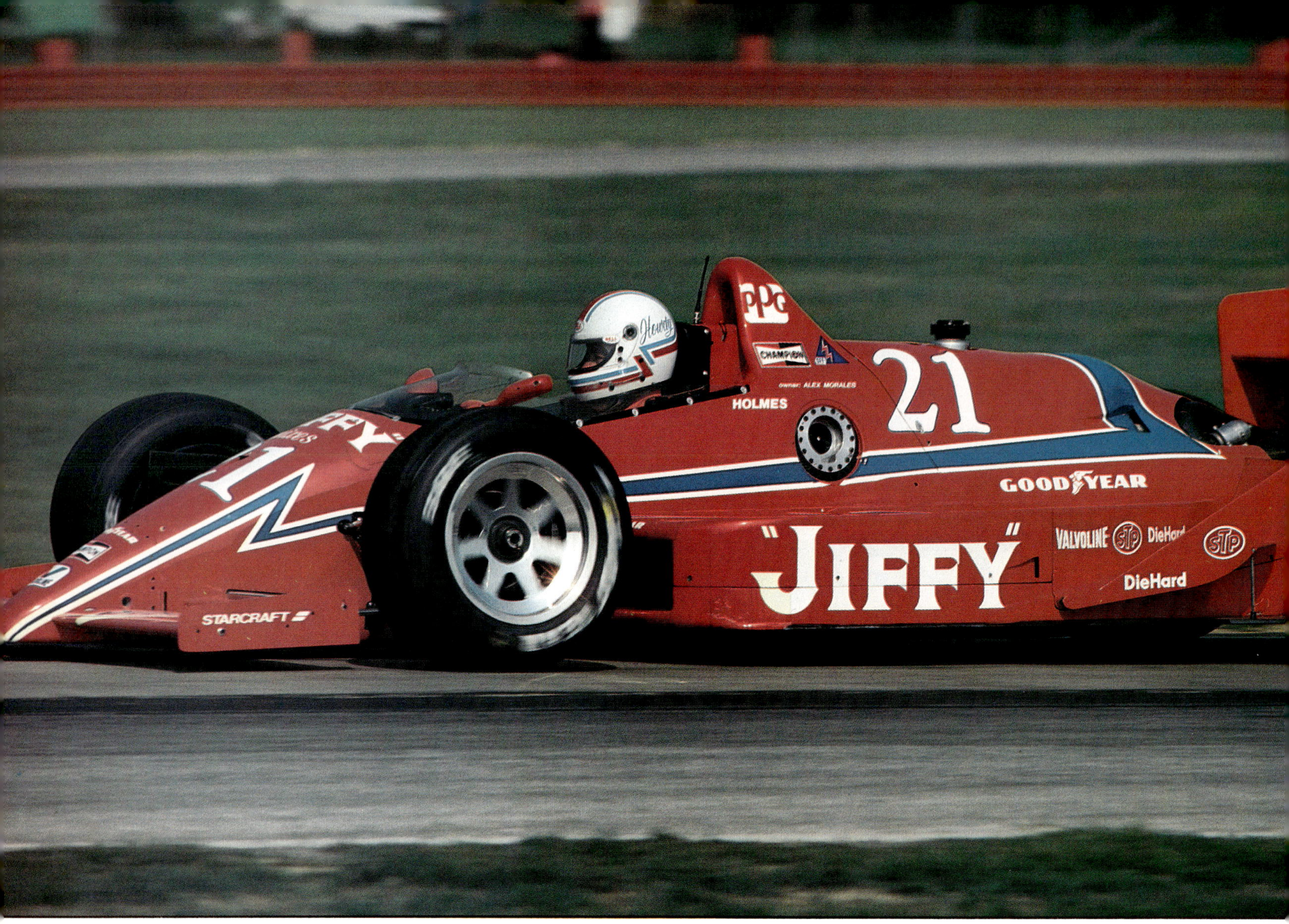

18 Howdy Holmes

EVENT	START	FINISH	PURSE	POINTS	TOTAL
Checker 200/Phoenix	16	10	$ 15,416	3	3
Toyota Grand Prix of Long Beach	22	17	17,150	0	3
Indianapolis 500	33	12	123,728	1	4
Miller High Life 200/Milwaukee	11	8	18,880	5	9
Budweiser/G.I. Joe's 200/Portland	19	16	16,680	0	9
Budweiser Cleveland Grand Prix	19	13	16,050	0	9
Molson Indy/Toronto	21	11	20,424	2	11
Marlboro Grand Prix/Meadowlands	13	23	16,120	0	11
Marlboro 500/Michigan	27	23	17,320	0	11
Quaker State 500/Pocono	18	7	21,219	6	17
Escort Radar Warning 200/Mid-Ohio	18	14	16,240	0	17
Briggs & Stratton 200/Elkhart Lake	19	11	16,374	2	19
Bosch Grand Prix/Nazareth	14	14	15,440	0	19
Champion 300km/Laguna Seca	20	23	14,120	0	19
Nissan Indy Challenge/Miami	20	8	22,480	5	24

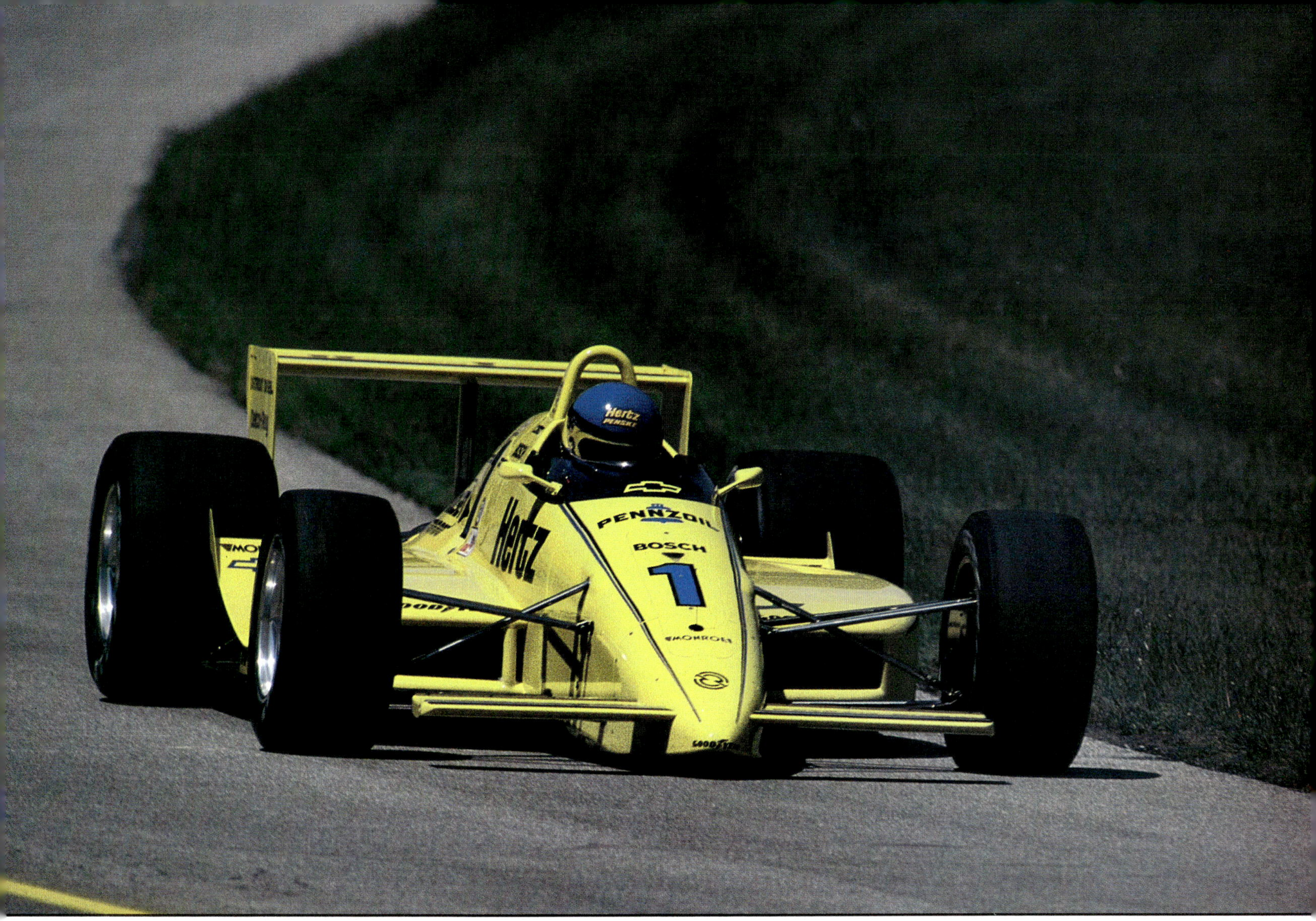

19 Al Unser

EVENT	START	FINISH	PURSE	POINTS	TOTAL
Checker 200/Phoenix	DNS			0	0
Toyota Grand Prix of Long Beach	DNS			0	0
Indianapolis 500	3	3	$228,403	14	14
Miller High Life 200/Milwaukee	DNS			0	14
Budweiser/G.I. Joe's 200/Portland	DNS			0	14
Budweiser Cleveland Grand Prix	DNS			0	14
Molson Indy/Toronto	20	9	21,360	4	18
Marlboro Grand Prix/Meadowlands	17	19	10,150	0	18
Marlboro 500/Michigan	2	9	15,808	4	22
Quaker State 500/Pocono	4	13	11,299	1	23
Escort Radar Warning 200/Mid-Ohio	DNS			0	23
Briggs & Stratton 200/Elkhart Lake	DNS			0	23
Bosch Grand Prix/Nazareth	DNS			0	23
Champion 300km/Laguna Seca	DNS			0	23
Nissan Indy Challenge/Miami	DNS			0	23

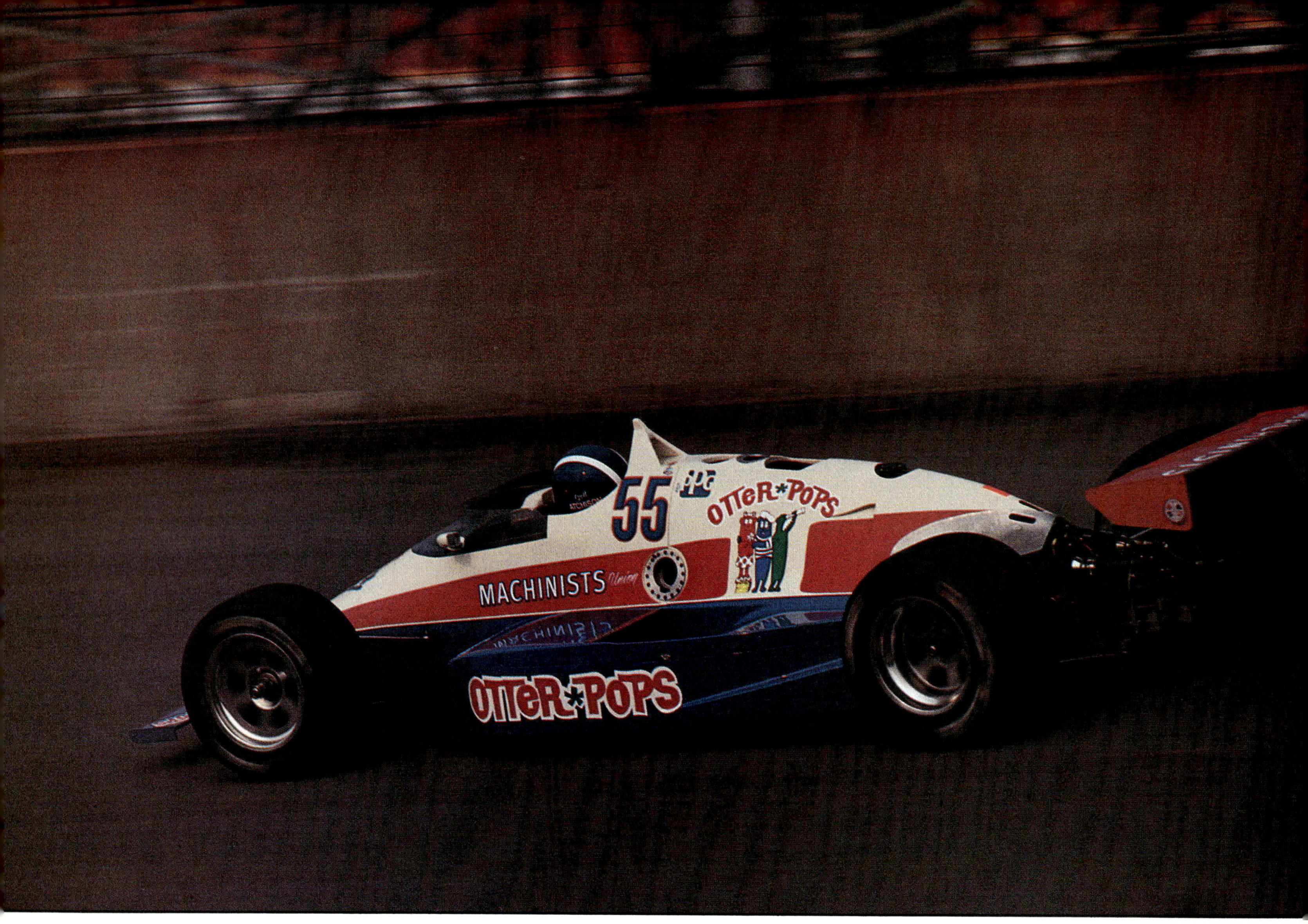

20 Scott Atchison

EVENT	START	FINISH	PURSE	POINTS	TOTAL
Checker 200/Phoenix	21	12	$ 15,050	1	1
Toyota Grand Prix of Long Beach	15	9	24,360	4	5
Indianapolis 500	DNS			0	5
Miller High Life 200/Milwaukee	15	16	14,580	0	5
Budweiser/G.I. Joe's 200/Portland	22	25	15,120	0	5
Budweiser Cleveland Grand Prix	25	12	11,050	1	6
Molson Indy/Toronto	22	13	19,800	0	6
Marlboro Grand Prix/Meadowlands	18	10	23,536	3	9
Marlboro 500/Michigan	25	10	22,024	3	12
Quaker State 500/Pocono	23	12	18,766	1	13
Escort Radar Warning 200/Mid-Ohio	20	15	16,240	0	13
Briggs & Stratton 200/Elkhart Lake	14	20	14,025	0	13
Bosch Grand Prix/Nazareth	DNS		7,000	0	13
Champion 300km/Laguna Seca	17	25	14,120	0	13
Nissan Indy Challenge/Miami	25	9	14,860	4	17

and when you look at AJ Foyt's age, my age, Bobby Rahal, Al Unser, Mario, you can eliminate 25% of today's field within the next 5 years."

He asked "Do you have a bunch of young drivers coming in right now? What car owners are helping the young drivers come in? What are they going to do when all of a sudden all of the older drivers are gone?"

Simon answered his own question "Somebody's got to do it. I'm not trying to be the hero of the association by any means. Diane and I are simply trying to make business sense out of our whole package."

The payoff is that sometimes through helping some of these other drivers we've opened different doors that have helped us on an overall basis. Perhaps not financially, so much, as it has in learning, in exposure, in being able to run a little bit more. If one of the drivers brings a sponsor, to cover at least half or more of the expenses, then that makes it possible for us to do a few miles that we wouldn't otherwise be able to do."

Ballabio came to Simon in 1987 and ran the Miami season finale. After the race Simon began to read brochures about ocean racing. "Being a race driver you get excited about racing anything, whether it's a soap box derby, Indy or a boat." So he asked "Hey, Fulvio, what's it take to race a boat?"

Fulvio's response was "You stay for one week of driving, if you steer ok; I'll let you race." according to Simon. Well, he did race but when comparing Indy racing to the other, "I think you have to be a little crazier driving the boat."

Ballabio, in turn, introduced Frey to Simon and gave up his ride at Laguna Seca and Miami to the handsome Swiss driver.

Then there is Tero Palmroth, who made his rookie debut at the Indianapolis 500 this year, a long way from his native Finland. Bill Simpson, of the fire suit fame, recommended Palmroth to the team. The original goal was a test session.

"We put together a program to come and test at Indy and Indianapolis Raceway Park, (a small road circuit) with no idea of running at Indy at all." But, "he did so well at IRP, he gained the speed very rapidly." Ever the entrepreneur, Simon asked Palmroth to talk to his sponsors. The money came through and Palmroth was enrolled at the Indianapolis Motor Speedway primary school, better known as the rookie tests, run weeks before official practice and qualifying.

"He was the fastest rookie the first day, and the fastest rookie the second day, so we took the car back to the shop and got it ready" for the main event the Indianapolis 500.

Ever the optimist, Simon conjectured "Had the engine not blown in the race he would have finished in the top 8."

Even established racers from other circuits get the bug sometimes to try something new. Geoff Bodine, originally from Chemung, New York, a Daytona 500 winning NASCAR driver, had raced just about every type of stock car but not an Indy car. Bodine was at the Michigan International Speedway for the IROC race and had the urge to try a 650 horsepower low slung racer just for the fun of it. Consider that CART/PPG Cup cars are somewhat faster and a lot more fragile than Winston Cup stockers.

This time it was not a young racer looking for his chance but a proven star in another branch of the sport. The catalyst was Dick Miller, of sponsor Provimi. Miller said to me "I realize it's not a rookie test and he could crash your car." Simon looked serious but responded "No, I don't think that Geoff's going to crash."

Then Simon warmed up a 1987 Lola by running laps of 210 and told him "the car is fine." On the fourth lap Bodine was 201 and his helmet was being pulled off because the windshield was too low for his height. Indy cars are just about custom made for the drivers. Bodine could drive a Lola, but, he couldn't sit in this one. The "test" ended with no one the worse for wear.

Bodine's fine run confirmed Simon's belief about race drivers. "You could take almost any good driver, whether it's NASCAR, Formula One, or any other circuit. If you prepare the car properly and he's smart enough to know not to do something radical" he could drive an Indy car.

Simon, as an owner of at least two cars, has had to learn something about adaptability. He elaborates, "There are only a few owner/driver combinations. Take AJ, he drives and owns, and he does a lot as far as the set up is concerned. He works directly with the team, no manager in between. You see him many times, out of the car, with a hammer in his hand. On the far side of the same situation you have Roger Penske, who used to be a driver. He knows a lot about cars as well as a lot about business. Roger plays a major role in making sure the communication from the drivers gets across to the mechanics. I think I do too."

At the season finale, in Miami, Luyendyk was running a strong second place when he retired, but, in Didier Theys' last rent-a-ride, Theys grabbed a third place for his temporary boss.

The tropical sunset was appropriate for ending the season and, perhaps, ending a phase in his life. Simon, who was the oldest man to compete in the Indianapolis 500, announced his retirement as a driver.

"It's time to put all my attention into making this team a winner. Maybe I've been trying to do too much," Simon explained, "Maybe, by taking myself totally out of the (driver's) seat, I can cover the little things that kept me out of the winner's circle."

For 1989, for the first time, Simon will have two "sponsored" cars, Luyendyk continuing in Provimi Veal livery, and Scott Brayton in Amway colors.

With Simon off the track and wearing headphones, he is ready to get his first win. Even if it's not as a driver, he can almost taste it. "I do think that when any time a team can knock on the door or come close, that is enough of a carrot to keep them going and keep the crew up."

Simon is one of the most "up" people on the CART circuit. Look out for the 1989 version of Dick Simon Racing.

Simon coaches Geoff Bodine (right).

PIT PARADE

RAYNOR RACING RECONNAISSANCE. Owner Ray Neisewander, Team Manager Bob Hancher, Driver Derek Daly and wife Beth Ann plot strategy at demanding Nazareth oval.

Amway's quick and personable young driver Scott Brayton with Amway's Rich DeVos who was on hand at Pocono to present his company's pole award.

Stroh's Chris Pfaus regularly jogged down pit lane following the fortunes of two Stroh Brewery backed cars, Rick Galles' March for Al Unser, Jr. (Stroh) and the Machinists Union's March for Kevin Cogan (Schaefer).

J. David Mackey, Marlboro Brand Manager, yellow shirt, was the center of attention from the electronic media prior to the start of Michigan's Marlboro 500.

PIT PARADE

CART's top pair, Chairman John Frasco and Executive Vice President John Caponigro (right) prior to the start of the Milwaukee round of the CART/PPG Championship.

Public Relations Director John Evenson's smile is well founded. Virtually every '88 CART race set a new attendance record.

CART's Assistant Operations/Technical Director Billy Kamphausen and Operations/Technical Director J. Kirk Russell.

Competition Director Wally Dallenbach details a fine point in the rules for Kevin Cogan.

PIT PARADE

OFF DUTY DRIVER... Out of the cockpit, Kevin Cogan sheds his Nomex coveralls for something more relaxing from Playboy Fashions. The shirt, in cotton blend sheeting by Stage II Apparel, and the jeans, by Sun Apparel, are from the '89 Playboy collection.

PIT PARADE

PPG Racing Director Jim Chapman chauffeurs Guerrero three year old, Marco, to hospitality area. If tradition holds, Marco will someday be seeking faster transportation, above. I.DE.A. Ferrari (below) brings an advanced Italian design concept and renowned Ferrari powerplant to the PPG pace car fleet. The $1 million plus "rolling laboratory" was accepted for PPG by Kears Pollock, Director, Automotive Original Finishes, left, from Ferrari North America top executives Hugh Steward and Emilio Anchisi. Roberto Barbiero, Ferrari Technical Director from Maranello is on the right.

PIT PARADE

Newman-Haas Racing's Paul Newman rests on pit row from his wagon-pulling chores.

Lola Cars' Eric Broadley, Michael Andretti and Newman-Haas Racing's Carl Haas survey the '89 Indy Car racing scene at Laguna Seca.

Horton Safety Team with comprehensively equipped GMC "instant response" truck.

Cheerful John Andretti perambulates pits in good form despite crutches, a memento of his Pocono encounter with unyielding wall.

PIT PARADE

SOUTH OF THE BORDER TO CELEBRATE...John Jones' father Tom, the '88 Rookie of the Year, Labatt's Glenn McPherson and Israel del Rio at Miami finale. Left, John Labatt's CEO Peter Widdrington.

TAKE HIGH PERFORMANCE DRIVING LESSONS
FROM THE MAN WHO WROTE THE BOOK...

He's the man whose driving school lists as graduates a cadre of CART front runners including Rick Mears and Al Unser, Jr.. His school was chosen by a platoon of entertainment world luminaries like Paul Newman, Robert Wagner, Clint Eastwood, and Gene Hackman, as well as corporate chief executives like Donald Petersen. He's paid his dues on the world's top race circuits, from Formula One and World Championship prototype sportscars to NASCAR stockers. His name is Bob Bondurant, his school is the Bob Bondurant School of High Performance Driving. You don't have to have Indy Car, film star or boardroom credentials to benefit, just a genuine desire to be a quicker, more secure, more confident driver. Courses range from a one-day Advanced Highway Driving course to a four-day Grand Prix course, and beyond. There's even an Anti-Terrorist course. Cars used range from Ford Mustang GT's to Crossle Ford single-seaters, or your own. If you drive at all, it's a rewarding investment in yourself, paying an extra dividend of pure enjoyment. IMSA approved. SCCA approved.

BOB BONDURANT™
SCHOOL OF HIGH PERFORMANCE DRIVING

HIGHWAYS 37 & 121
SONOMA, CA 95476
707-938-4741

OFFICIAL PRODUCTS: FORD CARS & TRUCKS   MOTORCRAFT PARTS   MERKUR XR4Ti

SPONSORS: GOODYEAR, KONI SHOCKS, CENTERLINE WHEELS, BELL HELMETS/RACE STAR SUITS, KONIG SEATS, BORG-WARNER TRANSMISSIONS

JOIN OUR TEAM
"SAY NO TO DRUGS"

A. J. FOYT
USAC, CART, NASCAR, IMSA

NEIL BONNETT
NASCAR

TERRY LABONTE
NASCAR

GREG SACKS
NASCAR

GEOFF BRABHAM
USAC, CART, IMSA

BOBBY RAHAL
USAC, CART, IMSA

MICHAEL ANDRETTI
USAC, CART, IMSA

CALE YARBOROUGH
NASCAR

Find out how **you** can join the team to help make America "drug-free." Call the National Federation of Parents for Drug-Free Youth at 1-800-55**4-KIDS**.

1989 CART/PPG INDY CAR WORLD SERIES SCHEDULE

April 9
CHECKER 200
Phoenix International Raceway, Phoenix AZ
April 16
TOYOTA GRAND PRIX OF LONG BEACH
Long Beach, CA
May 28
INDIANAPOLIS 500
Indianapolis Motor Speedway, Speedway, IN
June 4
MILLER HIGH LIFE 200
Wisconsin State Fair Park, West Allis, WI
June 18
DETROIT GRAND PRIX
Detroit, MI
June 25
BUDWEISER G.I. JOE'S 200
Portland International Raceway, Portland, OR
July 2
BUDWEISER CLEVELAND GRAND PRIX
Burke Lakefront Airport, Cleveland, OH
July 16
MARLBORO GRAND PRIX AT THE MEADOWLANDS
Meadowlands Sports Complex, E. Rutherford, NJ
July 23
MOLSON INDY TORONTO
Canadian National Exposition, Toronto, CAN.
August 6
MARLBORO 500
Michigan International Speedway, Brooklyn, MI
August 20
POCONO 500
Pocono Raceway, Long Pond, PA
September 3
MID-OHIO 200
Mid-Ohio Sports Car Course, Lexington, OH
September 10
BRIGGS & STRATTON 200
Road America, Elkhart Lake, WI
September 24
BOSCH SPARK PLUG GRAND PRIX
Pennsylvania International Raceway, Nazareth, PA
October 15
CHAMPION SPARK PLUG 300 KM
Laguna Seca Raceway, Monterey, CA

Off the track, the CART family is a large, and, for the most part, happy entourage. The rigors of traveling thousands of miles a year on a tight, 15 or 16 race schedule foster some close friendships, encourage sharing of responsibilities, and pitching in for the common cause. Quite often drivers' wives count other driver's wives as "best friends" despite their husband's rivalry on the track.

An impending family addition kept Shelley Unser away from the Miami race, failed to keep Al, Jr. out of the winner's circle.

Bobby Rahal's expanding family gets attention from the two-time CART/PPG Champion assisted by wife Debi.

Emerson Fittipaldi confers with daughters Juliana and Tatiana and son Jayson.

Michael and Sandra Andretti, of Nazareth, PA's first family.

CART FAMILY

Derek Daly and the smiling Irish eyes of wife Beth Ann, an Indiana native.

Rick's parents, Bill and "Skip" Mears, radiate approval of son's Indy 500 win.

The Kevin Cogans present their entry into the growing ranks of CART youngsters.

FOR THE RECORD

1988 PPG INDY CAR WORLD SERIES DRIVERS PERFORMANCE CHART

RANK	DRIVER	PTS	STS	RUN AT FIN.	TOP FIN	TMS LED	LAPS LED	LAPS COMP*	MILES COMP**	PURSE
1	DANNY SULLIVAN	182	15	11	1	24	517	1725	3133.932	$1,222,791
2	AL UNSER, Jr.	149	15	10	1	14	339	1591	3099.712	1,004,256
3	BOBBY RAHAL	136	15	13	1	7	71	1925	3510.200	867,093
4	RICK MEARS	129	15	11	1	15	475	1629	2907.673	1,414,472
5	MARIO ANDRETTI	126	15	7	1	17	240	1635	2870.037	712,091
6	MICHAEL ANDRETTI	119	15	11	2	3	3	1748	2987.423	887,187
7	EMERSON FITTIPALDI	105	15	7	1	12	231	1407	2556.632	942,636
8	RAUL BOESEL	89	15	9	4	2	6	1752	3098.099	597,052
9	DEREK DALY	53	15	8	4	0	0	1398	2487.354	436,230
10	TEO FABI	44	15	8	4	1	2	1217	1935.797	290,242
11	JOHN JONES	44	14	9	7	0	0	1579	2818.193	359,525
12	ROBERTO GUERRERO	40	12	5	2	0	0	1044	1859.366	345,706
13	KEVIN COGAN	40	11	5	3	0	0	1037	1795.934	369,424
14	ARIE LUYENDYK	31	15	5	2	4	86	1202	1961.770	403,732
15	DIDIER THEYS	29	8	5	3	0	0	547	1130.946	170,602
16	A.J. FOYT, Jr.	29	14	7	4	1	14	1259	2102.436	296,154
17	TONY BETTENHAUSEN	25	12	5	4	0	0	1285	2138.890	268,667
18	HOWDY HOLMES	24	15	11	7	0	0	1643	2988.473	374,641
19	AL UNSER	23	5	2	3	10	109	750	1627.001	320,020
20	SCOTT ATCHISON	17	13	8	9	0	0	1370	2427.651	235,531
21	GORDON JOHNCOCK	16	2	2	6	0	0	432	961.500	41,331
22	PHIL KRUEGER	15	4	3	5	0	0	547	1246.600	168,954
23	SCOTT BRAYTON	12	12	4	9	1	11	1110	1768.366	239,125
24	DICK SIMON	11	6	2	7	0	0	778	1446.000	212,944
25	ROCKY MORAN	9	10	4	6	0	0	740	1523.040	276,403
26	BERNARD JOURDAIN	8	2	1	6	0	0	137	256.878	28,370
27	JIM CRAWFORD	8	1	1	6	2	8	198	495.000	170,503
28	LUDWIG HEIMRATH, Jr.	7	9	2	7	0	0	523	986.271	240,803
29	RANDY LEWIS	7	14	4	9	0	0	1123	2185.903	328,866
30	BILLY VUKOVICH	6	4	3	9	0	0	688	1378.000	174,366
31	JOHN ANDRETTI	5	11	1	8	0	0	996	1713.114	268,068
32	RICH VOGLER	2	3	1	11	0	0	508	1191.500	144,488
33	DENNIS VITOLO	2	1	1	11	0	0	103	183.752	15,574
34	DALE COYNE	1	9	2	12	0	0	439	652.927	134,323
35	ED PIMM	1	2	1	12	0	0	115	330.900	18,540
36	KEN JOHNSON	1	1	1	12	0	0	77	170.478	17,300
37	JEAN-PIERRE FREY	0	2	1	13	0	0	84	182.536	13,575
38	SCOTT PRUETT	0	3	0	16	0	0	192	315.648	49,980
39	FULVIO BALLABIO	0	3	1	17	0	0	105	295.110	23,795
40	STEVE BREN	0	1	0	17	0	0	42	92.988	2,650
41	DOMINIC DOBSON	0	4	0	18	0	0	230	536.754	138,143
42	TERO PALMROTH	0	2	0	18	0	0	218	502.228	112,628
43	JOHNNY RUTHERFORD	0	2	0	18	0	0	236	525.500	116,907
44	DARIN BRASSFIELD	0	2	0	19	0	0	61	139.534	14,770
45	TOM SNEVA	0	2	0	22	0	0	125	266.000	114,805
46	DICK FERGUSON	0	1	0	22	0	0	19	31.730	4,120
47	STEVE CHASSEY	0	1	0	24	0	0	73	182.500	99,128
48	STAN FOX	0	1	0	30	0	0	2	5.000	113,703

*2112 laps available
**3809.112 miles available

ALL-TIME INDY CAR WORLD SERIES LEADERS

VICTORIES		POLE POSITIONS (1930-88)		LAP LEADERS (1946-88)		ALL-TIME EARNINGS	
1 A.J. FOYT, JR.	67	1 MARIO ANDRETTI	64	1 MARIO ANDRETTI	7159	1 MARIO ANDRETTI	$6,178,551
2 MARIO ANDRETTI	51	2 A.J. FOYT, JR.	53	2 A.J. FOYT, JR.	6621	2 AL UNSER	5,791,768
3 AL UNSER	39	3 BOBBY UNSER	49	3 AL UNSER	5797	3 RICK MEARS	5,684,137
4 BOBBY UNSER	35	4 AL UNSER	27	4 BOBBY UNSER	4862	4 BOBBY RAHAL	5,266,925
5 JOHNNY RUTHERFORD	27	5 RICK MEARS	26	5 GORDON JOHNCOCK	3417	5 DANNY SULLIVAN	4,255,444
6 RODGER WARD	26	6 JOHNNY RUTHERFORD	23	6 RODGER WARD	2955	6 JOHNNY RUTHERFORD	4,168,774
7 GORDON JOHNCOCK	25	7 GORDON JOHNCOCK	20	7 TONY BETTENHAUSEN	2869	7 AL UNSER, JR.	3,927,780
8 RALPH DePALMA	24	8 REX MAYS	19	8 JOHNNY RUTHERFORD	2703	8 TOM SNEVA	3,923,323
9 RICK MEARS	23	9 DON BRANSON	15	9 RICK MEARS	2653	9 A.J. FOYT, JR.	3,901,376
TOMMY MILTON	23	10 TOM SNEVA	14	10 BOBBY RAHAL	2007	10 MICHAEL ANDRETTI	3,596,878
11 TONY BETTENHAUSEN	21	TONY BETTENHAUSEN	14	11 TOM SNEVA	1781	11 GORDON JOHNCOCK	2,868,664
EARL COOPER	21	DANNY SULLIVAN	14	12 PARNELLI JONES	1589	12 EMERSON FITTIPALDI	2,859,638
13 JIMMY BRYAN	19	13 BOBBY RAHAL	13	13 JIMMY BRYAN	1290	13 BOBBY UNSER	2,674,516
JIMMY MURPHY	19	14 PARNELLI JONES	12	14 MICHAEL ANDRETTI	1238	14 ROBERTO GUERRERO	2,434,955
15 BOBBY RAHAL	18	15 RODGER WARD	11	15 DANNY SULLIVAN	1201	15 KEVIN COGAN	2,302,907
16 RALPH MULFORD	17	DANNY ONGAIS	11	16 DANNY ONGAIS	1073	16 GEOFF BRABHAM	2,108,434
17 TOM SNEVA	13	17 JOHNNY THOMSON	10	17 JOHNNY THOMSON	910	17 PANCHO CARTER	1,798,561
18 JOHNNIE PARSONS	11	DAN GURNEY	10	18 WALLY DALLENBACH	864	18 DICK SIMON	1,712,226
EDDIE HEARNE	11	19 JUD LARSON	9	19 AL UNSER, JR.	809	19 JOSELE GARZA	1,704,372
DANNY SULLIVAN	11	BILL CUMMINGS	9	20 MIKE MOSLEY	780	20 ARIE LUYENDYK	1,583,694
21 LOUIS CHEVROLET	10	21 LLOYD RUBY	8	21 DON BRANSON	751	21 GARY BETTENHAUSEN	1,403,240
PETER DePAOLO	10	JACK McGRATH	8	22 JOHNNIE PARSONS	731	22 RAUL BOESEL	1,367,124
FRANK LOCKHART	10	23 BOB SWEIKERT	6	23 LLOYD RUBY	728	23 SCOTT BRAYTON	1,222,013
DARIO RESTA	10	MICHAEL ANDRETTI	6	24 ROGER McCLUSKEY	723	24 HOWDY HOLMES	1,214,099
25 AL UNSER, JR.	8	TEO FABI	6	25 BILL VUKOVICH	713	25 DEREK DALY	1,190,871
LOUIS MEYER	8	26 EMIL ANDRES	5	26 JOE LEONARD	678	26 TONY BETTENHAUSEN	1,136,887
REX MAYS	8	PAUL RUSSO	5	27 BOB SWEIKERT	676	27 DANNY ONGAIS	1,056,169
EDDIE SACHS	8	ROBERTO GUERRERO	5	28 DAN GURNEY	643	28 MIKE MOSLEY	1,039,175
29 HARRY HARTZ	7	29 MIKE NAZARUK	4	29 EMERSON FITTIPALDI	567	29 WALLY DALLENBACH	1,033,701
JOHNNY THOMSON	7	DON FREELAND	4	30 ROBERTO GUERRERO	524	30 ROGER McCLUSKEY	1,012,346
LLOYD RUBY	7	SHORTY CANTLON	4	31 KEVIN COGAN	237	31 GEORGE SNIDER	921,039
DAN GURNEY	7	MARK DONOHUE	4	32 PANCHO CARTER	223	32 TEO FABI	906,006
EDDIE RICKENBACKER	7	GREG WELD	4			33 BILL VUKOVICH, JR.	882,213
MICHAEL ANDRETTI	7	BILLY ARNOLD	4			34 JIM McELREATH	844,054
		EDDIE SACHS	4			35 ED PIMM	821,716

On behalf of its
Owners, Drivers,
Teams and Sponsors,
Championship Auto Racing Teams
Honors the
1988 PPG Cup
National Champion
DANNY SULLIVAN

SULLIVAN AWARDED PPG CUP

Bruce Jenner hands '88 PPG Cup winner Danny Sullivan his personal replica of the huge trophy, foreground. PPG's Director of Racing, Jim Chapman, right, stands by with the $300,000 check that accompanies the trophy. Team owner Roger Penske, left, accepts *his* replica of the Cup, sharing the limelight with his entire team. Others in the top 20 drivers ranking gained awards in the $1.2 million PPG point fund as shown.

PPG CUP POINT FUND

1	Danny Sullivan	$300,000	11	John Jones	$20,000
2	Al Unser, Jr.	200,000	12	Robert Guerrero	16,000
3	Bobby Rahal	150,000	13	Kevin Cogan	12,000
4	Rick Mears	125,000	14	Arie Luyendyk	10,000
5	Mario Andretti	100,000	15	Didier Theys	8,500
6	Michael Andretti	65,000	16	A.J. Foyt	8,000
7	Emerson Fittipaldi	55,000	17	Tony Bettenhausen	7,500
8	Raul Boesel	45,000	18	Howdy Holmes	7,000
9	Derek Daly	35,000	19	Al Unser	6,000
10	Teo Fabi	25,000	20	Scott Atchison	5,000

AWARDS BANQUET

Additional Awards to Sullivan:
STP National Champion Award, $7,000
DeVilbiss Finish Line Award, $10,000
From PPG: A New Buick Reatta
The National Championship Ring
 (duplicate to Penske)

Additional Awards to Others:
Master Mechanic National Championship Award, $10,000; Chuck Sprague
AC Delco Top Three Drivers Award; $20,000
Vandervell Engine Builder Award, $15,000; VDS Racing
Rookie of the Year, Jim Trueman Memorial Trophy, $50,000; John Jones
STP Most Improved Driver Award, $3,000; A.J. Foyt
Master Mechanic Most Improved Award, $5,000; Owen Snyder
PPG Refinish Award, $10,000; STP/Granatelli Racing

Runner-up Al Unser, Jr. wore rabbit ears in a tribute to the errant bunny that blunted his Laguna Seca charge. Second place in the point fund was worth $200,000, a figure Al, Jr. described as "neat".

Unelko's Dave Ohlhausen, left, backed three Rain-X-embossed cars on the circuit, hosted a congenial front row table at the sold-out, 1600 guest CART Awards banquet. His rain repellent formula was in big demand over the Miami weekend which featured a subtropical deluge.

STP/Granatelli Racing garnered PPG Award for best use of color.

Chevrolet delegation clustered around Danny Sullivan's car included Bob Emerick, Frank Ellis, Herb Fishel, Fred Schaafsma and John Monk, cheered "bowtie brigade" drivers who copped five of the top seven places on the points list. Don Runkle, GM VP, is in center.

Out of uniform but very much in fashion, the PPG pace car drivers.

'89 OUTLOOK

CANADIAN JOHN JONES NAMED ROOKIE OF THE YEAR
Moves to Protofab for '89 Title Chase

Jim Trueman

The first two oval track races of the year demonstrated to young John Jones, the rookie driver in Frank Arciero's tightly knit team, just how tough Indy Car racing can be. At Phoenix he started 19th, finished 20th. At Indianapolis, after a frustrating 30 days, he didn't even start, a disappointment that could have been crushing to the talented 23 year old with an outstanding record in Formula 3000 and IMSA. For the rest of the season, young Jones demonstrated how tough *he* could be. At Milwaukee he exhibited an improving grasp of the difficult oval track technique still new to him. He started 17th and moved up 3 places at the finish. Next on the calendar came 4 road circuits, the type on which he had been so carefully schooled. Midfield qualifying and 8,7,7,7 finishes gave promise that Jones was a young driver of consistency belying his years.

Up next, two of the demanding ovals, superfast Michigan and super-difficult Pocono. Jones tamed them both. From far back grid positions he hauled down highly respectable 8th place finishes, went onto Mid-Ohio to forge a streak of seven consecutive top ten performances. While the remainder of the season saw him marginally outside first ten finishing positions, his overall total of 44 points tied that of Teo Fabi, a vastly more experienced chauffeur, and beat those of Roberto Guerrero, Arie Luyendyk, A.J. Foyt and Kevin Cogan, all recognized front rank drivers.

He was the clear cut choice for CART's 1988 "Rookie of the Year", the first winner of the Jim Trueman Memorial Trophy and the $50,000 cash award that accompanies it.

For '89 he'll be moving to the Protofab team, taking with him the Labatt's sponsorship that has fostered his career from the start. This leaves Frank Arciero the opportunity to choose as his driver another potential "Rookie of the Year." Arciero could make it three in a row.

THE CANADIAN CONNECTION:
JOHN JONES' ROAD FROM THUNDER BAY TO ROOKIE OF THE YEAR

Despite his obvious talent and intelligent approach, John Jones' success as the top first year driver on the '88 CART/PPG circuit almost certainly wouldn't have happened without the backing of a spirited, entrepreneurial group of Canadian businessmen who have nurtured his rapidly blossoming career. Started by his father Tom, an ardent club racer and Thunder Bay, Ontario, construction company owner with a friend, Richard Andison, head of Powell Equipment, Ltd., a heavy machinery company, the Jones Racing Limited Partnership quickly enlisted a platoon of major Canadian businessmen. The first of these were Montegu Black, president of Txibanguan Ltd. and James Connacher, CEO of Gordon Capital Co. Next came Trevor Eyton, CEO of Brascan Ltd., a major Canadian holding company. Others were Charles Cipolla, president of Controlled Media, John Finlay, president of Yorkborough Management Ltd. and Richard Bonnycastle, chairman of Cavendish Ltd. One of the partners, John Rhynas, president of Rhynas Holdings Inc., pitches in regularly as tire man on Jones' crew. He's known as the "Eagle Catcher", a reference to the Goodyears he fields.

This imposing group attracted other prominent Canadian business figures and raised sponsorship from Labatt's, Canada's largest brewery. Labatt's made possible Jones' two successful seasons in Formula 3000, the European series that is to Formula One what ARS is to CART. This experience was the platform that enabled young Jones to step directly into the demanding CART circuit, again with Labatt's backing.

After taking down rookie honors in '88, Jones will be back in a Labatt's Blue car in '89, taking aim at his next objective, becoming a full-fledged member of the exclusive front-runners club.

His backers have had their investment returned many times over in the pleasure of watching a personable young countryman fight his way up the ladder. Someday they may even get their money back.

STRICTLY STOCK PONTIAC

1980 Trans Am

The 20th Anniversary Trans Am GTA selected as the official pace car for the seventy-third running of the Indianapolis 500 not only has the specifications of a champion at 250 turbo-boosted horsepower and 340 ft. lbs. of torque, but the bloodlines as well. It's a direct descendant of the 1980 Trans Am which paced the "500" ten years earlier. The 1980 model was a prime example of the muscle car era and so much in demand that orders came from as far away as Saudi Arabia and the Arab Emirates.

Along the way some improvements have been made. As Mike Losh, Pontiac's General Manager puts it. "When our Trans Am paced this event in 1980, we modified the car to meet track requirements by simply leaving off the air conditioning package. Now, we have achieved the ultimate Trans Am to date with this 20th Anniversary Indianapolis 500 Pace Car...a completely stock car to pace these powerful racing machines!"

Losh noted that all fifteen hundred 20th Anniversary Trans Am GTAs

'89 OUTLOOK

20th Anniversary Trans Am GTA

TRANS AM PACES INDY 500

will actually be Indianapolis 500 Pace Cars. Any of them could be taken directly from the plant to the track and pace the race. In fact, the three vehicles required for on-Speedway driving will be picked at random and then specially fitted with Speedway-required safety lighting equipment. The 3.8 liter V-6 turbocharged Trans Am GTA models conceived to celebrate the special 20th birthday of this classic American muscle car, meet every Speedway performance requirement for pacing the race without any mechanical or technical modifications.

The car comes with a four speed automatic transmission and limited slip differential. Only option is the hatch roof that all Speedway-bound cars are equipped with. Since the '89 Trans Am GTA meets the exacting Speedway pace car requirements in stock form (and uses only a fraction of the fuel consumed by its 1980 predecessor), it is unlikely that any of the 1500 limited run will linger long in the marketplace.

Mike Losh

'89 OUTLOOK

PENSKE RACING operated in '88 like the Rolex ever present on the team owner's wrist. Six victories, the CART/PPG Championship, the Indianapolis 500, all with an "in house" chassis so good that it's a hot item on the "used car" market. What do you do for an encore after a season like that? More of the same; Mears and Sullivan driving, Al Unser invited for the 500 milers, Chevrolet in the engine bay *and* the PC-18. An anonymous member of the team called the all-conquering PC-17 "a nice little interim chassis"... If this is the case, the racing world can hardly wait to see the 18.

RICK GALLES and AL UNSER, JR... THE SECOND TIME AROUND

In admitting that it might have been an error in judgement to let a young driver with true star quality in his bloodlines and in his on-track performance slip away, Rick Galles reveals a strength of his Team Valvoline operation. Satisfied with nothing but the most competitive components, the Galles team corrects imperfections. As quickly as possible (in this case it took a couple of years) Rick Galles reclaimed for the '88 season the rapidly maturing star to whom he had given his first Indy ride. The results were spectacular. Al, Jr., always one of the quickest and most aggressive drivers on the circuit, became one of the winningest, his four victories matched only by new champion Danny Sullivan. But for an off-limits rabbit at Laguna Seca which induced front wing damage, he might have been able to put some real heat on Sullivan in the stretch drive for the CART/PPG Cup. The Galles/Unser partnership ended the season in a subtropical blaze of glory by romping home in front in the Miami finale, earning second place in the CART/PPG World Series of Auto Racing. The well matched pair sum it up this way...

Galles: *"If I had known in 1984 what I know now, I never would have let Al, Jr. leave the team. Al, Jr. has the force of personality that makes everybody around him better. He knows what it takes to be successful. I feel he's the best overall driver in the CART/PPG Series."*

Unser, Jr.: *"When Rick and I went our separate ways it was like breaking up a family. Since then, I've become a more mature driver and Rick has become one of the top Indy Car owners in the series. The chemistry is there for big things to happen. You could call it an old romance that's coming on stronger the second time around."*

For the coming '89 season, Galles Racing is placing its emphasis on research and development. Galmer Engineering Ltd., a new British company formed by Rick Galles and his chief engineer, Al Mertens, will be fully operational by the first of the new year. Galles is convinced, on the basis of his '88 experience, that a separate R&D facility is necessary to remain competitive. John Anderson remains as team manager. A switch to Lola chassis is in the works and the Chevrolet Indy V8 continues as the powerplant. Al Unser, Jr. is in the second year of a three year driving contract. With these key elements in place, Galles hopes to move up that all important notch from second place to the top. Unser, Jr.'s '89 car number, 2, is one that was good to daddy Al in the past.

STEVE HORNE PUTS SCOTT PRUETT IN TRUESPORTS' DRIVER'S SEAT FOR '89…

With the departure of two-time CART/PPG Champion and '88 runner-up, Bobby Rahal, to Kraco for a reported $1 million a year retainer, Truesports' Steve Horne had no lack of candidates for the vacant driving seat in his smartly run team. The choice; young and promising Scott Pruett, possessor of a Trans-Am championship, an IMSA GTO championship, a rare Formula One super license (unused) and only limited experience in an Indy Car. Horne's logic: "We're an American team. We wanted an American driver. Scott's a stand out. He tested well in our car. His off-track performance is as impressive as his driving. He has good road racing experience and we can teach him to handle the ovals. We've done that before."

Horne elaborated: "Although my background is in Formula One, on road circuits, I've come to have a great deal of respect for ovals. Ovals require a superior technique. They demand more finesse, more consistency. Mistakes are more costly. While Scott will be learning ovals in '89, I predict he'll win a road race."

In his three Indy Car outings Pruett has qualified respectably (13th at Long Beach, 16th at Meadowlands, 8th at Mid-Ohio) but has yet to finish in the points. Steve Horne, an exponent of consistency, is counting on major improvement in that category with Truesports' smooth operation behind the young driver.

On the team's '88 record, which fell just short of a 3rd consecutive championship, Horne observed.

"Penske had one big advantage, not better drivers not a better team, but better control of "resources." Having his own chassis and being able to concentrate on building 4 or 5 of these for a single customer, not 30 or 40 for a variety of customers, made the difference. At some point, we might have to start building our own cars from scratch instead of merely improving them."

On Truesports' future, Horne is looking to the 90's, counting on a young driver with championship potential, Judd engines with still unexplored boundaries ('89 will be the second year of a three year development program), and the momentum of his polished organization. As a parting shot Horne, who's so often been right in the past, had an observation on the world racing scene, "Don't be too surprised to see Indy Car racing and Formula One in some kind of a merger within the next five years."

'89 OUTLOOK

KRAINES RECRUITS RAHAL...

For a figure reported in the enthusiast press as $1 million per annum, Maury Kraines has signed Bobby Rahal, the 1986/87 CART/PPG Champion, who was in contention for the '88 title right up to the next to last race. "We're thrilled to have Bobby," states Kraines, "and prepared to pay in proportion to his accomplishments. We're not blaming Michael (Andretti) for our failure to win in '88, but the change should be good for everybody. We're going to go with Lola again and with Cosworth, which should benefit from a new development program. In the first three quarters of the season it was no fun to chase Chevrolets. In the last two races, we had an improved Cosworth and ran it with good results. Under the present rules, the Indy Car has almost reached its peak but there are still advances to be made in the engine. With Bobby's consistency and more horsepower, we're looking forward to a winning season." **Bottom photo shows Kraines and Rahal in discussion on the '89 season, the top one after Rahal switched hats.**

NEWMAN/HAAS NAMES MICHAEL ANDRETTI TO TWO-CAR TEAM

Mario Andretti has just about done it all in motorsports, won more money than any other Indy Car Driver, a World Championship in Formula One, and sportscar victories by the score. For '89 he'll be getting some special help in his endeavours. Son Michael will join him as co-equal no. 1 driver in a two car Newman/Haas team backed by retailing giant K mart. This "dream team" had been discussed before. However, Mario's posture was that it had its best chance of success when Michael had well and truly established himself as a driver in CART's elite "front runners" club. Michael again confirmed his status in this group by winning the '88 Marlboro Challenge where he was pitted against CART's best.

'89 OUTLOOK

DICK SIMON RACING: Simon gains the proven driving talents of Scott Brayton, shown with backer Amway's Bill Blaesing at the Miami event. This move puts two "young tigers" in the Simon stable (Arie Luyendyk is the other.), both of whom were in the handful of non-Chevrolet powered lap leaders in '88. Simon's racing philosophy is that if you can lead, you can win. With Simon calling the plays and leaving the cockpit chores to his youth movement, '89 could be the magic year. At Indianapolis Brayton bettered his own stock block record, four Buick powered laps at a 212.625 mph average.

Detroit Grand Prix

June 16, 17, 18, 1989

Features CART Indy Cars

The 8th running of this classic race through the streets of downtown Detroit will headline America's premier racing series, the CART/PPG World Series of Indy Car Racing. Fresh from the Indianapolis 500 will come America's best known racing stars... Stars with names like Andretti, Unser, Mears and Sullivan. The cars are the fastest turbo-charged single-seaters on the world's racing circuits, cars like the one that set a closed course world record of 233.934 mph. To share in the *new* excitement racing through the streets, call **Detroit Renaissance Grand Prix** at 313-259-5400.

89 OUTLOOK

Newest addition to the '89 CART/PPG calendar is the Detroit Grand Prix, June 16, 17, and 18, 1989. Indy Cars will use essentially the same downtown circuit around Renaissance Center as did Formula One cars for seven years. Governor James J. Blanchard, Mayor Coleman A. Young and Detroit Grand Prix President Robert E. McCabe (above) inspect the circuit in advance of the first appearance of the Indy Car contingent in downtown Detroit. Detroit area executives, some of whom have direct involvement in the Indy Car scene, reacted favorably. K mart Chairman Joseph Antonini, shown below, presenting the "Blue Light Special" trophy to driver Mario Andretti, Paul Newman and Carl Haas of the Newman/Haas Team which K mart backs put it this way: "What better place to run the prime American race car circuit than in the motor capitol of the world! It will be a great program for the city of Detroit. We at K mart are particularly pleased. It will be an opportunity for us to generate maximum exposure of the cars we'll sponsor in '89 for Mario and Michael Andretti."

THE CHEVROLET INDY V8, OUTLOOK FOR '89...

When queried about off season development for the all conquering '88 Chevrolet Indy V8, Fred Schaafsma's raised eyebrows set the tone for his reply, "Off-season?" There is no "off-season" in Indy engine development," stated Chevrolet's Chief Engineer. "The competition is too tough. We're at it all year, in season and out. So is our opposition, particularly after the year Chevy had in '88. Judd made a lot of progress, and actually put Rahal in the points lead with only three races to go. Steve Horne is highly competent and in '89 he'll only be in the second year of a three year (development) program with Judd. Cosworth may have been complacent when they had no competition. They're complacent no longer, are going to work closely with some leading teams, Porsche's engineering staff has an enviable record. They're not going to be satisfied just leading a race as they did this year. Next year Alfa Romeo will be a player. Not a bad player either, if you consider that they probably have access to the engine Ferrari put together for their own Indy Car project a while back.

We're going to do our best to stay on top of all the competition, competition which should make '89 a battle royal in the engine arena. We plan to put particular effort on electronic fuel management.

If you consider the limitations that CART puts on racing engines (no more than 8 cylinders, only 1 turbocharger, no intercooler) electronic fuel management is one of the few areas open for exploitation. Mechanical fuel injection systems only allow you to "bracket" ideal conditions. With the electronic route you can be right on target, vary your approach for the torque needed on road courses or the pure horsepower required for superspeedways. Moreover, the team engineer can get a reading while the race is going on and issue instructions to the driver on the track. We'll again be enlisting the aid of some of our sister GM divisions to supply components. It's good for them as well as for Chevrolet. We get top talent, they get the excitement of involvement in a fast moving sport and the discipline that goes with racing. For racing, every element in a system has to incorporate the best design, be manufactured to the highest quality standards, and be delivered on schedule. The starter's flag won't wait for next year's model to come out."

Nor, be assured, will Fred Schaafsma.

'89 OUTLOOK

RAYNOR GOES WITH JUDD

While most key elements of the successful '88 team remain in place for '89, Raynor Motorsports will switch to Judd engines for the new season. Raynor will share equally in the expanded second year development directed by Truesports' Steve Horne. Under new Team Manager Ray Neisewander III, driver Derek Daly, Chief Mechanic Kim Green, and Engineer John Ward are looking forward to improve on Raynor's '88 record, a ninth place in PPG points and a spot in the year end Marlboro Challenge. Team owner Ray Neisewander noted that Lola chassis will again be utilized and be the subject of an intensive pre-season testing and development schedule.

ALFA GOES INDY CAR RACING

No stranger to high performance... Juan Manuel Fangio drove a Tipo 159 Alfetta to his first world championship ...Italy's Alfa Romeo has announced its intention to have an Indy Car engine ready in time for the '89 Indianapolis 500. Highly successful Cesare Fiori will have oversight of the project. He is chief of parent FIAT's racing operations. The Lancia/Martini & Rossi rallye teams under his supervision have won the last two World Rallye Championships. Giorgio Pianta, chief of racing operations at Alfa Romeo, has visited the U.S. with a team of engineers to study the project. Alfa won't be starting from scratch; they have the bottom half of the Ferrari V8 developed for Indy but never used and are expected to build a completely new powerplant on this strong base.

1988 VALVOLINE CHAMPIONSHIP FOR BOSCH-VOLKSWAGEN SUPER VEE

"Rookie of the Year" Ken Murillo became "Driver of the Year" as well, when he notched the Drivers Championship with a record breaking 194 points. As a rookie champion, Murillo joined illustrious company. Al Unser, Jr., the only other driver to turn the trick, was a four time winner on the CART/PPG circuit this season, beaten in the points parade only by Champion Danny Sullivan. Since the stated objective of the series (after providing fast, affordable single-seater racing) is to produce competent new driving talent for the Indy Car circuit, Super Vee had a banner year. Volkswagen Motorsports Director Michael Kaptuch noted that every Super Vee champion since 1980 campaigned in this year's CART/PPG circuit. Among recent "graduates" to join the Indy Car arena this year were Scott Atchison, who scored 17 PPG Cup points, Bernard Jourdain with 8, Dennis Vitolo with 2, Ken Johnson 1 (in his first outing) and Steve Bren.

E.J. Lenzi took home the honors as '88's "Most Improved" Super Vee driver. His ten top finishes and 163 points made him the runner up in the Valvoline Championship. Lee Hagen, in charge of Murillo's car, was named "Best Mechanic", and Dave Conti took home honors as "Most Improved" Mechanic. Hagen now has produced three Drivers Champions in five years, the other pair being Arie Luyendyk (a CART/PPG standout) and Ken Johnson. With over 1.1 million people viewing full fields of Super Vee action in '88, the health of the series seems assured.

MURILLO WINS DEBUT AT PHOENIX...

Ken Murillo, in his first Super Vee race, won Sunday's Valvoline Championship for Bosch-Volkswagen Super Vee series season opener at Phoenix International Raceway.

Murillo took the lead on the 17th lap and never relinquished it, winning going away. Murillo's final margin of victory was a whopping 12.48 seconds over second place finisher Mark Dismore. Danny Hill, Jr., also running in his first Super Vee race, finished third.

The race was marred by a four car crash that finished the day's racing for then leader and polesitter Mark Smith, his brother and fellow front row qualifier, Mike Smith and the Jourdain brothers, Bernard and Michel.

"I only know how to drive one way—as fast as the car will go," said the victorious Murillo.

Murillo, last year's Barber-Saab champion, had only a two race agreement with the Lee Hagen Racing team coming into the race, but chances are that will be extended after his performance Sunday.

As unexpected as Murillo's victory was, the most surprising events of the day were the finishes of Dismore and Hill. Dismore hadn't even secured a ride a week before the race, while Hill's main goal coming into the race was just to finish.

1988 VALVOLINE CHAMPIONSHIP FOR BOSCH-VOLKSWAGEN SUPER VEE RACE 1
Checker 200, Phoenix, AZ
April 10, 1988
60 Laps of 1 Mile Circuit for 60 Miles

FIN.	ST.	DRIVER	CAR	PTS.	PURSE
1	3	KENNY MURILLO	Lee Hagen Ralt RT-5	20	$6,500
2	7	MARK DISMORE	Conti Ralt RT-5	16	4,600
3	8	DANNY HILL, JR.	Racing Dynamics Ralt RT-5	14	3,400
4	6	E.J. LENZI	Turtle Wax Ralt RT-5	12	2,250
5	20	ROBERT GROFF	Groff Ralt RT-5	11	1,900
6	14	STUART CROW	Earl's Supply Ralt RT-5	10	1,600
7	18	PETER J. PITTMAN	Fan Grabber Vicky Walt PJ3	9	1,350
8	9	PAT PHINNY	Baja Cantina Ralt RT-5	8	1,200
9	22	STEPHEN A. WULFF	Bradley Ralt RT-5	7	1,000
10	19	RICHARD DELORTO	Chicago Divorce Assoc. Ralt RT-5	6	900

RADISICH WIRE TO WIRE AT LONG BEACH...

Polesitter Paul Radisich led from start to finish to win the second round of the Valvoline Championship for Bosch-Volkswagen Super Vee at the Toyota Grand Prix of Long Beach.

Radisich, who was also on the pole for last year's Long Beach event, won by a 3.05 second margin over Robbie Groff. In the past two years the talented Radisich has picked up two firsts, two seconds and an eighth in his only five Super Vee starts.

"I knew if I got through the first corner in front, I'd have it," Radisich said. "For the first 10 laps, I felt a little tight, so I told myself to relax."

Groff, last season's "Rookie-of-the-Year" in Super Vee competition, started Sunday's race second on the grid and his second place finish was his best career Super Vee finish.

"I was happy just to keep up with him (Radisich) the first few laps," Groff said. "He was just a notch better."

Murillo, last week's winner in his Super Vee debut at Phoenix, finished fourth—good enough to retain sole position of first place in the Drivers Championship with 33 points after two rounds. Groff's second moved him up to second overall with 27 points.

1988 VALVOLINE CHAMPIONSHIP FOR BOSCH-VOLKSWAGEN SUPER VEE RACE 2
Toyota Grand Prix of Long Beach, Long Beach, CA
April 17, 1988
37 Laps of 1.67 Mile Circuit for 61.79 Miles

FIN.	ST.	DRIVER	CAR	PTS.	PURSE
1	1	PAUL RADISICH	Ralt American Ralt RT-5	20	$6,500
2	3	ROBERT GROFF	Groff Ralt RT-5	16	4,600
3	2	BERNARD JOURDAIN	Cimarron Ralt RT-5	14	3,400
4	5	KEN MURILLO	Lee Hagen Ralt RT-5	12	2,250
5	9	MARK SMITH	Dave White Ralt RT-5	11	1,900
6	6	JOHN C. BROOKS	Hasa/Brooks Ralt RT-5	10	1,600
7	13	CHRIS SMITH	Earl's Supply Ralt RT-5	9	1,350
8	14	MIKE SMITH	Ralt American Ralt RT-5	8	1,200
9	15	STEVE WULFF	Bradley Ralt RT-5	7	1,000
10	12	PAT PHINNY	Baja Cantina Ralt RT-5	6	900

SUPER VEE

JOURDAIN DAZZLES IN DALLAS...

Bernard Jourdain took the lead on lap 31 and never relinquished it. He went on to register his first Valvoline Championship for Bosch-Volkswagen Super Vee victory by 18.548 seconds over second place Paul Radisich at the inaugural Grand Prix of Dallas.

Jourdain, of Mexico City, started the race on the front row next to polesitter Radisich and waged a battle with the New Zealander for the lead. He passed Radisich once, but was unable to hold the lead after missing a gear. He regained his composure, repassed Radisich and ran away from the field.

Radisich, coming off a victory at Long Beach, led for 67 straight laps in the Super Vee series over two races in two different cars. He won the Long Beach Super Vee in a Ralt American ride and came back in Dallas with the Dave Conti Racing team. Radisich had visions of a second consecutive win before Jourdain and some clutch problems brought that to an end.

E.J. Lenzi moved up to third early and ran a consistent race to his highest finish of the young season.

1988 VALVOLINE CHAMPIONSHIP FOR BOSCH-VOLKSWAGEN SUPER VEE RACE 3
Pontiac Grand Prix of Dallas, Dallas, TX
May 1, 1988
50 Laps of 1.2 Mile Circuit for 60 Miles

FIN.	ST.	DRIVER	CAR	PTS.	PURSE
1	2	BERNARD JOURDAIN	Cimarron Ralt RT-5	20	$6,500
2	1	PAUL RADISICH	Conti Ralt RT-5	16	4,600
3	9	E.J. LENZI	Turtle Wax/Baci Ralt RT-5	14	3,400
4	5	KEN MURILLO	Lee Hagen/Kegl Ralt RT-5	12	2,250
5	10	STEVE KNAPP	Dave White Ralt RT-5	11	1,900
6	15	MARK SMITH	Dave White Ralt RT-5	10	1,600
7	13	CHARLES NEARBURG	McNeill Ralt RT-5	9	1,350
8	8	RICK HILL	Carlos Bobeda Ralt RT-5	8	1,200
9	12	JOHN C. BROOKS	Brooks Racing Ralt RT-5	7	1,000
10	14	STUART CROW	Earl's Supply Ralt RT-5	6	900

MIKE SMITH WINS "NIGHT BEFORE THE 500" SUPER VEE...

Mike Smith, driving the Ralt American Ralt RT-5, passed polesitter E.J. Lenzi on lap 52, then went on to win the Budweiser "Night Before the 500" race.

Smith, a McMinnville, OR native and a junior at the University of Washington, picked up his first career Super Vee victory by a 7.51 second margin over Lenzi, the 1987 winner at I.R.P. Smith turned in an average speed of 112.540 mph, breaking the previous I.R.P. standard. Lenzi was the only other driver in the field on the same race lap.

Robbie Groff led the first 15 laps of the race after getting a great jump on Lenzi on the green flag, but Groff's car wasn't able to hold up and Lenzi took the lead on lap 16. Lenzi looked like he was on his way to capturing his second consecutive I.R.P. victory, leading laps 16-51. Smith had other ideas, though, as he made a fine move on turn three of lap 52 to take a lead he would never relinquish. Smith's victory gave his Ralt American team its second victory of the season, after former teammate Paul Radisich won the Grand Prix of Long Beach.

1988 VALVOLINE CHAMPIONSHIP FOR BOSCH-VOLKSWAGEN SUPER VEE RACE 4
"Night Before the 500", Indianapolis, IN
May 28, 1988
80 Laps of .686 Mile Circuit for 54.88 Miles

FIN.	ST.	DRIVER	CAR	PTS.	PURSE
1	3	MIKE SMITH	Ralt American Ralt RT-5	20	$6,500
2	1	E.J. LENZI	Turtle Wax/Baci Ralt RT-5	16	4,600
3	4	KEN MURILLO	Lee Hagen Ralt RT-5	14	3,400
4	5	BERNARD JOURDAIN	Cimarron Ralt RT-5	12	2,250
5	7	ROBERTO QUINTANILLA	Cimarron Ralt RT-5	11	1,900
6	6	MARK SMITH	Dave White Ralt RT-5	10	1,600
7	2	ROBERT GROFF	Groff Ralt RT-5	9	1,350
8	8	PETER J. PITTMAN	Fan Grabber Vicky Walt PJ3	8	1,200
9	12	BEN BARTEL	Griffith/Griffith GR06	7	1,000
10	11	STEVE THOMSON	Gillund Ralt RT-5	6	900

GROFF WINS FIRST AT "MILWAUKEE MILE"...

Robert Groff, of Northridge, CA, dominated every aspect of the racing weekend to win his first career Valvoline Championship for Bosch-Volkswagen Super Vee race at the Wisconsin State Fair Park Speedway.

Groff, the 1987 Super Vee "Rookie of the Year", earned his first Super Vee pole position on Saturday. He then led from start to finish with E.J. Lenzi and Mike Smith, respectively, the only other racers on the lead lap. Groff also turned in the fastest race lap by touring the one mile oval in 28.330 seconds for a speed of 127.073 mph.

"I had an absolutely perfect car today," said the 22 year old Groff. "I just went and carried out my crew chief's orders."

1988 VALVOLINE CHAMPIONSHIP FOR BOSCH-VOLKSWAGEN SUPER VEE RACE 5
Miller 200, Milwaukee, WI
June 5, 1988
62 Laps of 1 Mile Circuit for 62 Miles

FIN.	ST.	DRIVER	CAR	PTS.	PURSE
1	1	ROBERT GROFF	Groff Ralt RT-5	20	$6,500
2	2	E.J. LENZI	Turtle Wax/Baci Ralt RT-5	16	4,600
3	4	MIKE SMITH	Ralt American Ralt RT-5	14	3,400
4	3	MIKE HOOPER	Dave White Ralt RT-5	12	2,250
5	7	BERNARD JOURDAIN	Cimarron Ralt RT-5	11	1,900
6	5	KEN MURILLO	Provimi Veal/Hagen Ralt RT-5	10	1,600
7	8	PAUL RADISICH	Conti Ralt RT-5	9	1,350
8	6	MARK SMITH	Dave White Ralt RT-5	8	1,200
9	12	STEVE WULFF	Bradley Ralt RT-5	7	1,000
10	13	PETER J. PITTMAN	Fan Grabber Vicky Walt PJ3	6	900

RADISICH REPEATS IN DETROIT...

Paul Radisich, of Auckland, NZ, continued his street circuit domination of the Valvoline Championship for Bosch-Volkswagen Super Vee as he led from start to finish for the second straight year to win the Detroit Grand Prix Super Vee event.

Radisich earned his third pole position of the year on Saturday and was never headed on Sunday. In the process, Radisich set two Detroit records. His overall speed of 75.944 mph and his first race lap of 1:56.494 (77.332 mph) both set new standards for the race run through the streets of Detroit.

Radisich became the first driver to win two races in the Super Vee series this season, having captured the Long Beach title in another start-to-finish victory earlier this year.

E.J. Lenzi picked up his third consecutive second place finish right behind Radisich. Had anyone other than Radisich occupied the pole, Lenzi just might have been in the winner's circle, as he consistently turned in lap times faster than the previous record.

1988 VALVOLINE CHAMPIONSHIP FOR BOSCH-VOLKSWAGEN SUPER VEE RACE 6
EniChem Detroit Grand Prix, Detroit, MI
June 19, 1988
24 Laps of 2.5 Mile Circuit for 60 Miles

FIN.	ST.	DRIVER	CAR	PTS.	PURSE
1	1	PAUL RADISICH	Conproco/Conti Ralt RT-5	20	$6,500
2	3	E.J. LENZI	Turtle Wax/Baci Ralt RT-5	16	4,600
3	8	KEN MURILLO	Lee Hagen Ralt RT-5	14	3,400
4	5	CHRIS SMITH	Earl's Supply Ralt RT-5	12	2,250
5	9	PAT PHINNY	Baja Cantina Ralt RT-5	11	1,900
6	11	STUART CROW	Ralt American Ralt RT-5	10	1,600
7	10	ROBERTO QUINTANILLA	Cimarron Ralt RT-5	9	1,350
8	13	JIM WARD	Jim Ward/Duraflame Ralt RT-5	8	1,200
9	18	LEE PERKINSON	Open Pit Ralt RT-5	7	1,000
10	17	KENNETH WELD	Complete Engines/Weld Ralt RT-5	6	900

RADISICH WINS NIAGARA GRAND PRIX FOR TWO IN A ROW...

Paul Radisich picked up his second consecutive win and his third of the season by copping the Niagara Falls event. 2.253 seconds separated him from Ken Murillo at the finish.

Radisich, starting on the front row for the fourth time in six races this season, now has four wins and four seconds in eight career races held on street circuits. Radisich established the race record for (63.567 mph) and fastest race lap (71.756 mph) through the streets of Niagara Falls.

Radisich took the lead on lap three and only Murillo could keep pace with the 24 year old Kiwi. Yet, Radisich felt he could have asked for more from the Conproco/Dave Conti Racing Ralt RT-5.

1988 VALVOLINE CHAMPIONSHIP FOR BOSCH-VOLKSWAGEN SUPER VEE RACE 7
Niagara Falls International Grand Prix, Niagara Falls, NY
June 26, 1988
37 Laps of 1.6 Mile Circuit for 59.2 Miles

FIN.	ST.	DRIVER	CAR	PTS.	PURSE
1	2	PAUL RADISICH	Conti Ralt RT-5	20	$6,500
2	3	KEN MURILLO	Lee Hagen Ralt RT-5	16	4,600
3	12	BERNARD JOURDAIN	Cimarron Ralt RT-5	14	3,400
4	8	MARK SMITH	Dave White Ralt RT-5	12	2,250
5	21	ROBERT GROFF	Groff Ralt RT-5	11	1,900
6	18	E.J. LENZI	Turtle Wax/Baci Ralt RT-5	10	1,600
7	5	STUART CROW	Ralt American Ralt RT-5	9	1,350
8	7	MIKE SMITH	Ralt American Ralt RT-5	8	1,200
9	7	ROBERTO QUINTANILLA	Cimarron Ralt RT-5	7	1,000
10	4	STEVE WULFF	Bradley Ralt RT-5	6	900

SUPER VEE

RADISICH ON A ROLL TAKES BUDWEISER CLEVELAND GRAND PRIX...

Paul Radisich notched his third consecutive victory and his fourth of the season by winning the Budweiser Cleveland Grand Prix Super Vee event by 0.709 seconds over Bernard Jourdain.

Radisich made a spectacular move on the race's first lap as he shot from his fourth place starting position into the lead on turn six of the 11 turn course. He and Jourdain then battled wheel-to-wheel over the last 15 laps of the race.

Jourdain made the first move as he passed the New Zealander on lap 12 and went on to open up a three second lead. Radisich wasn't through, though, as he bided his time until an opening presented itself on lap 23. Radisich spotted the opening and seized the lead.

1988 VALVOLINE CHAMPIONSHIP FOR BOSCH-VOLKSWAGEN SUPER VEE RACE 8
Budweiser Grand Prix, Cleveland, OH
July 3, 1988
25 Laps of 2.48 Mile Circuit for 62 Miles

FIN.	ST.	DRIVER	CAR	PTS.	PURSE
1	4	PAUL RADISICH	Conti Ralt RT-5	20	$6,500
2	3	BERNARD JOURDAIN	Cimarron Ralt RT-5	16	4,600
3	1	ROBERT GROFF	Groff Ralt RT-5	14	3,400
4	6	KEN MURILLO	Lee Hagen Ralt RT-5	12	2,250
5	2	MARK SMITH	Dave White Ralt RT-5	11	1,900
6	5	MIKE SMITH	Ralt American Ralt RT-5	10	1,600
7	7	E.J. LENZI	Turtle Wax/Baci Ralt RT-5	9	1,350
8	8	CHRIS SMITH	Earl's Supply Ralt RT-5	8	1,200
9	12	STEVE WULFF	Bradley Ralt RT-5	7	1,000
10	9	STUART CROW	Ralt American Ralt RT-5	6	900

MARK SMITH NAILS DOWN FIRST WIN AT MEADOWLANDS...

Mark Smith of McMinnville, OR, took the lead on lap 10 and never looked back as he drove his Evergreen Aviation/Dave White Motorsports Ralt RT-5 to victory in the Valvoline Championship for Bosch-Volkswagen Super Vee race at the Marlboro Grand Prix—Meadowlands by 9.579 seconds over E.J. Lenzi's Turtle Wax Ralt RT-5.

1988 VALVOLINE CHAMPIONSHIP FOR BOSCH-VOLKSWAGEN SUPER VEE RACE 9
Marlboro Grand Prix, Meadowlands, E. Rutherford, NJ
July 24, 1988
50 Laps of 1.2 Mile Circuit for 60 Miles

FIN.	ST.	DRIVER	CAR	PTS.	PURSE
1	4	MARK SMITH	Evergreen/Dave White Ralt RT-5	20	$6,500
2	9	E.J. LENZI	Turtle Wax/Baci Ralt RT-5	16	4,600
3	6	CHRIS SMITH	Earl's Supply Ralt RT-5	14	3,400
4	2	KEN MURILLO	Lee Hagen Ralt RT-5	12	2,250
5	11	STEVE WULFF	Bradley Ralt RT-5	11	1,900
6	12	RUSS WICKS	Dave White Ralt RT-5	10	1,600
7	14	JIM WARD	Duraflame/Jim Ward Ralt RT-5	9	1,350
8	17	FRANK CHIANELLI	Arbco Wheels Ralt RT-5	8	1,200
9	10	ROBERTO QUINTANILLA	Laredo Bank/Cimarron Ralt RT-5	7	1,000
10	13	DUANE MAY	Haggar Apparel/Sunbelt Ralt RT-5	6	900

MURILLO MARCHES AT MID-OHIO...

Rookie Ken Murillo of Santa Rosa, CA, took the lead from E.J. Lenzi on lap 11, and was never headed in his Lee Hagen Racing Ralt RT-5 for a 14.88 second victory at the Mid-Ohio Sports Car Course.

The race was run under dry conditions after qualifying in a steady rain on Saturday. Polesitter Paul Radisich and second fastest qualifier Bernard Jourdain collided on the first lap. This gave Lenzi and Murillo a chance to slide by into the first two positions. Murillo and Lenzi battled for the lead for the first 11 laps of the race. Murillo finally passed Lenzi on lap 11 and was never seriously threatened during the 25 lap, 60 mile affair.

1988 VALVOLINE CHAMPIONSHIP FOR BOSCH-VOLKSWAGEN SUPER VEE RACE 10
Escort 200, Lexington, OH
September 4, 1988
25 Laps of 2.4 Mile Circuit for 60 Miles

FIN.	ST.	DRIVER	CAR	PTS.	PURSE
1	3	KEN MURILLO	Lee Hagen Ralt RT-5	20	$6,500
2	5	E.J. LENZI	Turtle Wax/Baci Ralt RT-5	16	4,600
3	1	PAUL RADISICH	Conproco/Conti Ralt RT-5	14	3,400
4	8	ROBERT GROFF	Groff Ralt RT-5	12	2,250
5	2	BERNARD JOURDAIN	Cimarron Ralt RT-5	11	1,900
6	4	MIKE SMITH	Evergreen/Ralt American Ralt RT-5	10	1,600
7	12	ROBERTO QUINTANILLA	Laredo Bank/Cimarron Ralt RT-5	9	1,350
8	17	JIM WARD	Duraflame/Jim Ward Ralt RT-5	8	1,200
9	11	JOHN C. BROOKS	Hasa Chemical/Brooks Ralt RT-5	7	1,000
10	10	MARK SMITH	Evergreen/Dave White Ralt RT-5	6	900

GROFF DOMINATES ROAD AMERICA...

Robert Groff of Northridge, CA, led from start-to-finish to win the Road America Super Vee event in Elkhart Lake, WI. It was his second victory of the season as he bested Ken Murillo by a margin of 9.76 seconds.

Groff's victory capped off a weekend in which he turned in the fastest time of every Super Vee session. Groff secured the pole on Saturday with a 111.008 mph lap and then turned the fastest race lap at over 109 mph in Sunday's triumph.

1988 VALVOLINE CHAMPIONSHIP FOR BOSCH-VOLKSWAGEN SUPER VEE RACE 11
Briggs & Stratton 200, Elkhart Lake, WI
September 11, 1988
15 Laps of 4 Mile Circuit for 60 Miles

FIN.	ST.	DRIVER	CAR	PTS.	PURSE
1	1	ROBERT GROFF	Groff Ralt RT-5	20	$6,500
2	9	KEN MURILLO	Lee Hagen Ralt RT-5	16	4,600
3	4	BERNARD JOURDAIN	Cimarron Ralt RT-5	14	3,400
4	6	E.J. LENZI	Turtle Wax/Baci Ralt RT-5	12	2,250
5	11	PAUL RADISICH	Conproco/Conti Ralt RT-5	11	1,900
6	8	STUART CROW	Ralt American Ralt RT-5	10	1,600
7	7	CHRIS SMITH	Earl's Supply Ralt RT-5	9	1,350
8	15	STEVE THOMSON	Gillund Ralt RT-5	8	1,200
9	2	MARK SMITH	Evergreen/Dave White Ralt RT-5	7	1,000
10	12	ROBERTO QUINTANILLA	Laredo Bank/Cimarron Ralt RT-5	6	900

MURILLO NAILS DOWN NAZARETH, SUPER VEE TITLE...

Ken Murillo of Santa Rosa, CA, became the first rookie since Al Unser, Jr., in 1981 to win the Valvoline Championship for Bosch-Volkswagen Super Vee Driver's Championship. He won his third Super Vee race of the season at Pennsylvania International Raceway to clinch the title.

1988 VALVOLINE CHAMPIONSHIP FOR BOSCH-VOLKSWAGEN SUPER VEE RACE 12
Bosch Spark Plug Grand Prix, Nazareth, PA
September 24, 1988
60 Laps of 1 Mile Circuit for 60 Miles

FIN.	ST.	DRIVER	CAR	PTS.	PURSE
1	2	KEN MURILLO	Murillo/Lee Hagen Ralt RT-5	20	$6,500
2	9	BERNARD JOURDAIN	Cimarron Ralt RT-5	16	4,600
3	5	E.J. LENZI	Turtle Wax/Baci Ralt RT-5	14	3,400
4	4	MIKE SMITH	Evergreen/Ralt American Ralt RT-5	12	2,250
5	3	MARK SMITH	Evergreen/Dave White Ralt RT-5	11	1,900
6	7	STUART CROW	Wyndham's/Ralt Amer. Ralt RT-5	10	1,600
7	8	BEN BARTEL	American Thunder Ralt RT-5	9	1,350
8	10	PAUL RADISICH	Conproco/Conti Ralt RT-5	8	1,200
9	11	JIM WARD	Duraflame/Jim Ward Ralt RT-5	7	1,000
10	12	JOHN C. BROOKS	Hasa Chemical/Brooks Ralt RT-5	6	900

JOURDAIN WINS FINALE AT ST. PETERSBURG, MURILLO SETS RECORD...

Bernard Jourdain, of Mexico City, led 26 of 30 laps to win his second race of the season at the GTE St. Petersburg Grand Prix. He shared the spotlight with new Driver's Champion Ken Murillo, a rookie who established a new Super Vee record for most points in a season.

Jourdain who made his successful CART/PPG Indy Car debut last weekend at Laguna Seca, defeated second place Murillo by 1.647 seconds. He averaged 73.824 mph over the 30 lap, 60 mile circuit through the streets of downtown St. Petersburg. His earlier victory this season was also on a street course (the Grand Prix of Dallas).

Murillo, the 23 year old series champion, surpassed Scott Atchison (now a regular on the CART/PPG Indy Car circuit). His second place finish gave him 194 points for the season, five more than Atchison's 1987 record total. The record capped off a Cinderella season.

Murillo adds his name to an impressive list of Super Vee champions.

1988 VALVOLINE CHAMPIONSHIP FOR BOSCH-VOLKSWAGEN SUPER VEE RACE 13
GTE Grand Prix, St. Petersburg, FL
October 22, 1988
30 Laps of 2 Mile Circuit for 60 Miles

FIN.	ST.	DRIVER	CAR	PTS.	PURSE
1	1	BERNARD JOURDAIN	Cimarron Racing Ralt RT-5	20	$6,500
2	3	KEN MURILLO	Lee Hagen Racing Ralt RT-5	16	4,600
3	4	ROBERT GROFF	Groff Ralt RT-5	14	3,400
4	5	E.J. LENZI	Turtle Wax/Baci Ralt RT-5	12	2,250
5	11	STUART CROW	Ralt American Ralt RT-5	11	1,900
6	14	KENNETH WELD	Complete Engines/Weld Ralt RT-5	10	1,600
7	17	JIM WARD	Duraflame/Jim Ward Ralt RT-5	9	1,350
8	19	TOM VANCAMP	Griffith Motorsports Griffith GR06	8	1,200
9	23	LEE RACKLEY	Rackley Motorsports Ralt RT-5	7	1,000
10	12	STEVE THOMSON	Gillund Enterprises Ralt RT-5	6	900

AL UNSER, JR. GETS THE JUMP, BAGS BUDWEISER IROC TITLE...

Al Unser, Jr., heeding his father's advice to "Get the Jump", won the final IROC round at Watkins Glen and the series record $211,900 that went with the title. In so doing he turned the tables on the polesitter and last year's champion Geoff Bodine, from nearby Chemung, NY. Bodine is the top level NASCAR pilot who last year "out jumped" Al, Jr. to take down the husky award and the '87 championship. As a two-time series titlest, Unser, Jr. is matched only by A.J. Foyt.

After his fast start, Al, Jr. prevailed despite three full course yellow flags which erased substantial leads, held on to finish 1.58 seconds ahead of Terry Labonte in the 30 lap, 72.84 mile chase around the 2.4 mile circuit. He averaged 110.924 mph.

In just three IROC series, Unser, Jr. has pocketed $470,000, easily out-distancing previous series record holder Cale Yarborough's total of $313,000 in eight IROC appearances.

Labonte's runner-up finish moved him into second place in the IROC standings with 55 points, 11 behind Unser, Jr. Labonte earned $95,000, while SCCA Trans-Am title-holder Scott Pruett, who finished third at the Glen, wound up third in the points with 51, worth $72,900.

Bodine's bid to take a second consecutive crown in the series which matches a dozen of the world's top drivers, representing different racing disciplines, in identically prepared IROC-Z Chevrolet Camaros equipped with Goodyear Eagle radial tires, ended when he slid off the track after 16 laps while running third. Trying to chase down Unser, Jr. he hit the guardrail. Although Bodine made it back to the pits, the car was too damaged to continue.

Unser, Jr., who now is tied for second place in IROC history with four race wins, immediately accepted an invitation from IROC Chairman Les Richter to defend his title next year.

Three-time LeMans winner Al Holbert finished fourth, followed by Al Unser, Chris Cord, Dale Earnhardt and Bill Elliott. Chip Robinson, who pitted, was ninth, one lap down, as was Bobby Rahal. Roberto Guerrero, who brought out the first full course yellow when he spun on lap 2, was eleventh and Bodine was 12th. Earnhardt caused the second caution period when he spun.

BUDWEISER INTERNATIONAL RACE OF CHAMPIONS

POINT STANDINGS AND BONUS MONEY

1. AL UNSER, JR., 66 points, $211,900
2. TERRY LABONTE, 55 points, $95,000
3. SCOTT PRUETT, 51 points, $72,900
4. BILL ELLIOTT, 46 points, $58,900
5. DALE EARNHARDT, 45 points, $51,000
6. GEOFF BODINE, 45 points, $49,500
7. AL HOLBERT, 39 points, $35,000
8. AL UNSER, 38 points, $34,000
9. CHIP ROBINSON, 36 points, $38,000
10. CHRIS CORD, 26 points, $32,000
11. BOBBY RAHAL, 24 points, $31,000
12. ROBERTO GUERRERO, 19 points, $30,400

HFC AMERICAN RACING SERIES
BEEKHUIS WINS TITLE FOR ARS BUICK POWERED CARS

Jon Beekhuis avoided a multiple car first lap crash that sidelined Jeff Andretti and two others, cruised to a comfortable 5th place and the season title on the restart in Miami. His closest pursuer in the points parade was Irishman and ex-Formula One driver Tommy Byrne, who won the season finale after a spirited duel with Juan Manuel Fangio III, nephew of the famed Argentinian World Champion. Fangio ended the season out of the top five despite some sparkling drives. Calvin Fish, the 3rd place Miami finisher was 4th in the season total, behind Dave Simpson of the Simpson Racing Equipment family. Ted Prappas was fifth on the points list.

Also in the field were Daniel Campeau of the noted Canadian department store family, Steve Shelton, the new Formula Atlantic Champion, Brian Ongais, son of the Indy Car driver.

After the race, at CART's awards dinner, Beekhuis took home $20,000 from the points fund, a 1989 Buick Regal and a free CART Indy Car test with Truesports.

ARS driver Jeff Andretti (2nd left) gets encouragement from other members of the clan: Mario, John and Michael.

Buick ARS engine is based on production pushrod unit.

HFC AMERICAN RACING SERIES

RACE #1   PHOENIX INT'L. RACEWAY APR. 9, 1988

FIN.	ST.	DRIVER	SPONSOR	PURSE
1	3	PAUL TRACY	Sherman Williams	$16,000
2	2	CALVIN FISH	HFC / Team Shierson	7,900
3	12	WALLY DALLENBACH, Jr.	Polyvoltrac / Colorado	3,900

RACE #2   WISCONSIN STATE FAIR PARK JUNE 4, 1988

FIN.	ST.	DRIVER	SPONSOR	PURSE
1	1	DAVE SIMPSON	Simpson Racing Prod.	$19,500S
2	2	MIKE SNOW	Chaz Cologne — Revlon	7,900
3	12	JOHN McCRAKEN	JMC Racing	3,900

RACE #3   PORTLAND INT'L. RACEWAY JUNE 19, 1988

FIN.	ST.	DRIVER	SPONSOR	PURSE
1	1	TOMMY BYRNE	Opar Racing	$19,500S
2	2	JUAN MANUEL FANGIO II	TEAMKAR Int'l.	7,900
3	3	JON BEEKHUIS	A.B.S.I. / P.I.G.	3,900

RACE #4   BURKE LAKEFRONT AIRPORT JULY 3, 1988

FIN.	ST.	DRIVER	SPONSOR	PURSE
1	1	JUAN MANUEL FANGIO II	TEAMKAR Int'l.	$21,500S
2	4	CALVIN FISH	HFC / Team Shierson	7,900
3	3	DAVE SIMPSON	Simpson Racing Prod.	3,900

RACE #5   TORONTO, ONT JULY 17, 1988

FIN.	ST.	DRIVER	SPONSOR	PURSE
1	2	CALVIN FISH	HFC / Team Shierson	$19,500
2	1	TOMMY BYRNE	Opar Racing	8,900S
3	5	GUIDO DACCO	Filtravedo	3,900

RACE #6   MEADOWLANDS COMPLEX JULY 24, 1988

FIN.	ST.	DRIVER	SPONSOR	PURSE
1	1	JON BEEKHUIS	Say No to Drugs	$19,500S
2	3	DAVE SIMPSON	Simpson Racing Prod.	7,900
3	4	TOMMY BYRNE	Opar Racing	3,900

RACE #7   POCONO INT'L. RACEWAY AUG. 20, 1988

FIN.	ST.	DRIVER	SPONSOR	PURSE
1	4	MICHAEL GREENFIELD	Greenfield Inds.	$19,500
2	3	TOMMY BYRNE	Opar Racing	7,900
3	1	DAVE SIMPSON	Simpson Racing Prod.	4,900S

RACE #8   MID-OHIO SPORTS CAR COURSE SEPT 4, 1988

FIN.	ST.	DRIVER	SPONSOR	PURSE
1	1	JON BEEKHUIS	Say No to Drugs	$19,000S
2	3	TOMMY BYRNE	Opar Racing	7,900
3	10	TED PRAPPAS	TEAMKAR Int'l.	3,900

RACE #9   ELKHART LAKE, WI SEPT 11, 1988

FIN.	ST.	DRIVER	SPONSOR	PURSE
1	2	JUAN MANUEL FANGIO II	Arciero Wines	$18,500
2	3	JON BEEKHUIS	Say No to Drugs	7,900
3	7	TED PRAPPAS	TEAMKAR Int'l.	3,900

RACE #10   PENN. INT'L. RACEWAY SEPT. 25, 1988

FIN.	ST.	DRIVER	SPONSOR	PURSE
1	1	CALVIN FISH	HFC / Team Shierson	$22,500S
2	2	MIKE GROFF	Paul Mitchell	7,900
3	4	MIKE SNOW	Chaz Cologne	3,900

RACE #11   LAGUNA SECA RACEWAY OCT. 16, 1988

FIN.	ST.	DRIVER	SPONSOR	PURSE
1	4	TOMMY BYRNE	Opar Racing	$19,500
2	3	JON BEEKHUIS	Say No to Drugs	7,900
3	1	JUAN MANUEL FANGIO II	Arciero Wines	4,900S

RACE #12   TAMIAMI PARK NOV. 6, 1988

FIN.	ST.	DRIVER	SPONSOR	PURSE
1	2	TOMMY BYRNE	Opar Racing	$17,000
2	1	JUAN MANUEL FANGIO II	Arciero Wines	8,900S
3	4	CALVIN FISH	HFC / Team Shierson	3,900

S — Includes $1,000 STP Pole Award

HFC FORMULA ATLANTIC CHALLENGE

Shelton Takes '88 Title, Toyota Invests $1.5 Million in the Series

Steve Shelton, last year's runnerup, nailed down his first Formula Atlantic title in St. Petersburg, took his no. 1 Swift into the Sebring finale "just for fun." He finished third after qualifying first. A pair of Scotts, Harrington and Goodyear, took down the first two Sebring slots. Harrington was third in the final standings behind J.O. "Jocko" Cunningham who distinguished himself as a potential Danny Sullivan by "spinning and winning" in the St. Petersburg round. John Thompson and Colin Trueman of the Truesports Truemans rounded out the top five.

Despite these accomplishments on the track, perhaps the biggest Atlantic news of the year was Toyota Motor Sales USA's announcement that it was providing a $1.5 million injection of fresh money into the series over a 3 year period.

A 1.6 liter, twin cam, multiple valve engine derived from the Corolla GTS and MR2 production engines will become the standard engine for the series. The race prepared version weighs in at 225 horsepower, will get on-site Toyota technical assistance. Toyota will make the engine available to qualified drivers at a subsidized price, provide additional support in the form of TV coverage, purse monies.

$1 MILLION CORVETTE CHALLENGE

Wolocatiuk takes St. Petersburg Finale. Hayner collects $100,000 Series Title

Mark Wolocatiuk romped home in St. Petersburg's season ending Corvette Challenge race for a $11,000 payday. Fifth place Stuart Hayner held off Juan Manuel Fangio III, his closest pursuer in the points race, to take the inaugural Corvette Challenge title, which was accompanied by a check for $100,000 from the half million dollar point fund. Hayner's season total was $142,800. Fangio's $115,300. Third place in the series went to Tommy Archer who posted winnings of $100,450, not bad for an ex-ice racer from Duluth. Fourth place Andy Pilgrim's season's efforts netted $67,200. Wolocatiuk notched fifth in the title chase, good for $62,050. He tied Archer for the $7,500 Goodyear pole position award worth $7,500.

The Corvette Challenge, organized by Canadian John Powell, and patterned after Canada's GM Player's Challenge, was an overnight success in its inaugural year. Everyone of the 50 identical stock Corvettes available for the series was snapped up by Chevrolet dealers who entered them for qualified drivers. Dealer Tom Bell's Mobil Team won the team competition. There was even a $25,000 award to the dealer who best promoted his racing activities. A committee which included Chevrolet's Bob Emerick, Frank Ellis, Dave McClellan and Ralph Kramer picked Bergstrom Chevrolet for the award. Bergstrom's driver, Mark Behm, finished 17th. Former Indy 500 winner turned sportscaster Johnny Rutherford won the sportsmanship award.

The format for the Corvette Challenge is geared for excitement. The top six qualifiers start in inverted order. K. C. Van Niman, a Procter & Gamble VP and longtime SCCA official, is Chief Steward for the series, which rigorously enforces the stock provisions in the rules. Only "add ons" permitted are those related to safety.

Another ten race series is on tap for '89. Half of these are slated for CART/PPG venues. Fifty '89 Corvettes will be set aside for the competition. No hold over cars will be allowed to enter. "The '89s are just too fast," reports series organizer Powell.

CORVETTE CHALLENGE DRIVER'S POINT STANDINGS, 10 RACE TOTALS

POS.	CAR NO.	DRIVER	SPONSOR/ENTRANT	POINTS
1	98	STUART HAYNER	Tom Bell/Mobil 1/Autosport	795
2	2	JUAN MANUEL FANGIO III	Manliba/Gloy Sports	778
3	34	TOMMY ARCHER	Nova/NB Ventures	725
4	18	ANDY PILGRIM	Princess Casinos/Bergstrom	714
5	8	MARK WOLOCATIUK	Miller Racing/Malcolm Konner	702
6	78	SHAWN HENDRICKS	MPS Mtrsprts/Valley Chevy	667
7	33	MARK DISMORE	DR Mtrsprts/Amoco/Nat'l Car	645
8	76	PETER CUNNINGHAM	MPS Mtrsprts/Valley Chevy	622
9	20	JIM VASSER	Rippie Racing/Amoco/Nat'l Car	595
10	36	BILL COOPER	DR Mtrsprts/Amoco/Nat'l Car	552
11	80	DOC BUNDY	Miller Racing/Malcolm Konner	549
12	95	BORIS SAID III	East Coast Exotic Cars	518
13	32	BOBBY ARCHER	Nova/NB Ventures	495
14	11	PETER LOCKHART	Rippie Racing/Bob Johnston	443
15	97	BOBBY CARRADINE	Tom Bell/Mobil 1/Autosport	425
16	12	LOU GIGLIOTTI	Keith Young Chevrolet	406
17	7	MARK BEHM	Bergstrom Racing	352
18	17	SCOTT LAGASSE	Jack Wilson Chevrolet	350
19	58	ROBIN DALLENBACH	CM Racing/Malcolm Konner	225
20	99	JOHNNY RUTHERFORD	Young Chevrolet	208
21	16	BRUCE JENNER	Cahill/Jenner/Gloy Racing	207
22	42	RANDY RUHLMAN	Performed Line Products	190
23	62	MITCH WRIGHT	Team Bergstrom	184
24	68	TOM KENDALL	Nova Racing	163
25	21	TONY PIOCOSTA	Racing USA	162
26	70	DESIRE WILSON	Malcolm Konner	161
27	44	ANDY EVANS	Arco/AM PM/'Vettes Unlimited	155
28	0	PAUL HACKER	Young Chevrolet	124
29	0	MAX JONES	Young Chevrolet	116
30	37	JEFF ANDRETTI	Rippie Racing/Bergstrom Racing	114
31	5	MIKE HUGHES	Precision Auto Centers	108
32	55	MIKE ENGELAGE	Panther Racing/E3 Racing	92
33	4	JOHN BRANDT	Frederick Chevrolet	88
34	66	CHARLES BISLAND	Genderson Chevrolet	79
35	3	BRAD MURPHEY	Gloy Sports	77